UNDER SHELL-FIRE

THE HARTLEPOOLS
SCARBOROUGH AND WHITBY
UNDER SHELL-FIRE

FREDERICK MILLER.

The Naval & Military Press Ltd

Published by

The Naval & Military Press Ltd

Unit 5 Riverside, Brambleside
Bellbrook Industrial Estate
Uckfield, East Sussex
TN22 1QQ England

Tel: +44 (0)1825 749494

www.naval-military-press.com
www.nmarchive.com

COLONEL L. ROBSON, R.G.A., C.M.G., D.S.O., V.D.
Commanding Durham R.G.A.
"Fire Commander," Hartlepool Batteries, Dec. 16th, 1914.

(See page 70)

CONTENTS.

APPENDIX.

PREFACE.

Though a mere incident in the greatest of all wars now being waged on the three continents of the Old World and on all the seas, yet the daring adventure which was followed by the bombardment of the three English coast towns is of historical importance, not only to the towns concerned, but to the country at large and to the Empire overseas. This will be conceded when it is recalled how large a sympathy it evoked, to say nothing of the world-wide surprise, indignation and anger it called forth. Having no direct effect upon the European struggle, this savage reprisal upon practically unfortified towns is a measure of the culture to which modernised Prussia has attained. All the naval facts connected with it cannot be known for some time, but it is essential to the future historian of the stupendous events of this period that he should have all that tragic forty-minutes' meaning at his command. For him, for the inhabitants of these stricken towns, for their relatives and friends at home and abroad this little book is written.

FREDERICK MILLER.

West Hartlepool,
     January, 1915.

I.

THE EAST COAST.

Thrice is he armed that hath his quarrel just;
And he but naked, though lock'd up in steel,
Whose conscience with injustice is corrupted.
                                        —*Henry VI.*

On its eastern coast Britain slopes away to the sea. On its western shores the sentinel mountains keep watch over the wild waves of the Atlantic, across which, some 3,000 miles, was a little more than four centuries ago the unchallenged home of the Red Man. Now, it is a new world in the making. The North Sea is part of the great moat unbridged, save by the stately ships which carry food and fare, nature's raw product and man's finished work, with man himself, hither and thither. The moat is the silver streak which surrounds the buttressed walls, the shelving slopes, the deep set inlets of our island home. On the other side of it, some 200 or 300 miles away, is the home of our Teutonic forefathers, against whose descendants we, emigrant children, are now waging relentless war. For, from the mouth of the Elbe, about Cuxhaven and Wilhelms-haven and the Kiel Canal, behind the scenes of which the German Navy awaits its turn, came the Anglo Saxons and the Danes, the former of whom made refugees of the ancient British occupiers and drove them to take shelter in the rock-built homes of the west. And not far from these came the hardy Norsemen in their oak-ribbed keels to ravage the East coast and to abide on its soil. The Normans were but an offshoot of these ruthless pirates. Under the first William they brought " Doomsday " to the Saxon farmer, the curfew's warning to extinguish the light, the men in shining armour to annex the loot. It is within the bounds of possibility that the last Wilhelm, who has before now come in the guise of a friend, may come again as greedy, as rapacious, as mail-fisted as William, the conqueror of the Saxons—if we leave the way open for his heaven-appointed mission.

East and South, Britain has been the prey of the Teutonic invader. It is to invasion that we owe the vigour of our

9

blood, the enterprise of our people, the strength that is in us to-day. The blood that is ours is a rich blend, purified through the centuries by the stern tonic of adversity as it is being purified now. But we need none of the later Teutonic strain. That is polluted by that upstart ambition by which even angels fell; by a contempt of that which is small and presumably weak; by a claim to ride rough-shod over the world and to leave not even standing room to any who bar the way to progress made in Prussia. The nations of Europe are bound to defend civilisation, as they know it, a civilisation of which they are proud. If not, Kaiser Wilhelm will suffocate them in an atmosphere of imperialism without right, justice or mercy—an imperialism which lays claim to dominate the world.

The east coast of Britain, with all its deviations and indentations is about 700 miles in length from the Orkneys to the South Foreland. This is the shore-line which was once cemented to continental Europe before what we now call the North Sea swept through, separated us from our neighbours and left us free. The great fortresses of the nations, like Port Arthur and Gibraltar, frown at the enemy at the gates of narrow seas. Land fortresses, like Coblentz, Metz, Strasburg, serve the purpose of the ancient watch-houses along the Roman wall. They are camps of concentration guarding the boundary line, the great gun emplacements around which are spread out the men and munitions against threatening war. The closest of neighbours are often the farthest from being fast friends. Germany was in such close touch with Denmark that she coveted and took the vineyard of Schleswig. Germany, determined to be the central master-power of continental Europe, invented the needle gun and laid Austria low. Germany in 1870 resolved that the time had come to humiliate France and then to bring within the imperial net all the smaller fry of German kingdoms, duchies and states. Much has happened since then. Diplomacy, the handmaid of deceit, has brought about a new grouping of the Powers. Old foes have become new friends. Wilhelm II, his professors and war-lords had, like Napoleon, fixed upon one master only for Europe. The modern Imperial Cæsar was the man. And so the Triple Entente was placed in the balance against the Triple Alliance. Had there been a Napoleon living, which there was not, Europe had no use for him. Like Jehu, the son of Nimshi, one might be found to drive furiously, but the race is not always to the swift nor the battle to the strong. Wilhelm II. could not suffer the steadying hand of Bismarck, and now he and Moltke have gone. Everything and everybody was to be Germanised, only German airs were to be played, only German air might be breathed. There was only one thing left to the world worth living for—the right of glorified Germany everywhere to reign.

Along those 700 miles of coastline of which we were speaking there is no fortress, no great place of arms in the ordinary acceptation of the term. Nature has given us the enveloping sea, and the sea is the home of our floating forts, the navy of our pride. "Punch," in his amusing way, gives a conversation between an old woman and her friends: "And what has become of Kruger now?" asks she. "There is no Kruger now; 'tis the Kaiser." "And so the old varmint 'as changed 'is name 'as 'e?" The Kaiser, at any rate, has an ever-changing character to fit in with time and place. We have seen him as a chief mourner following Victoria, our Queen; we have seen him hurl his Prussian Guards at her grandson's "contemptible" best. The War-Lord of Prussianised Germany constructed and widened the Kiel Canal as a naval base and mercantile short-cut between the North Sea and the Baltic. His famous telegram to Paul Kruger only resulted in Chamberlain mobilising the Channel Fleet. He saw our convoys of ships, men and supplies, traversing the Atlantic from Southampton to Table Bay, and he saw that in our Navy was a concentrated defensive power that no army of his could touch to its hurt. He resolved, at whatever cost, to build a fleet which in time should rival our own and make him not only disposer of the land but arbiter of the sea. So the canal with its Kiel harbour was completed and then deepened and widened. Britain, awake to the new position, began to establish the Rosyth base on the Firth of Forth, north, and Dover harbour on the south. Between these two fortified stations the East coast was practically unprotected.

Hartlepool has long since thrown off her ancient armour; her walls may still beat back the sea, but she is otherwise defenceless; her upstanding rocks have been toppled over by the encroaching tide. If Hartlepool was a defended port, West Hartlepool, like Scarborough and Whitby, was at the mercy of the attacking cruisers. German culture does not include mercy; "frightfulness" has taken its place. And then, these towns, like Rheims Cathedral, were in the line of German fire. Hartlepool has two small batteries of 6-in. guns, but what are they against shells fired several miles away? In much the same way the mouth of the Tees on the Yorkshire side is guarded by fort and garrison. But Britain here and Britain away was at war with Germany. The High Seas Fleet had taken cover out of sight and out of reach. It must do something to justify its existence. The whole of cultured Germany was out for blood, the blood especially of the much hated English-speaking race, who now stood in the path confronting the freebooters of central Europe. "Stand and deliver!" said the German. "Stand off that I may take your height!" said the Britisher. The height has been taken, the first throw won. The ultimate result, though hardly to be questioned, is yet in the hands of time. But Britain was at defensive war, Germany at aggressive murder. And so it came about that on a bright, sunny morning in December, when a lifting haze covered the sea, as it does sometimes in mellow autumn, when the wavelets just turned over on the limestone beach like the soft petals of white chrysanthemums, when half the world was only half awake, when the children were getting into their stride for school and the workman was looking for his breakfast—then the German vomit was thrown upon battery, beach, and the thickly peopled streets of the two Hartlepools, to defile, desecrate and destroy. But Britain was at war. And defenceless Scarborough and Whitby knew that Germany was not. She was simply providing a tonic for the jaded nerves of a disappointed people. To do it she was swift to shed blood. In forty minutes her might was manifested in killed and maimed to the number of more than five hundred! This was not war as waged by the knightly and chivalrous, but an inhuman lust for blood by a people to whom life was no longer sacred.

The "VON DER TAN," one of the Bombarding Fleet.
(*see page 129*)

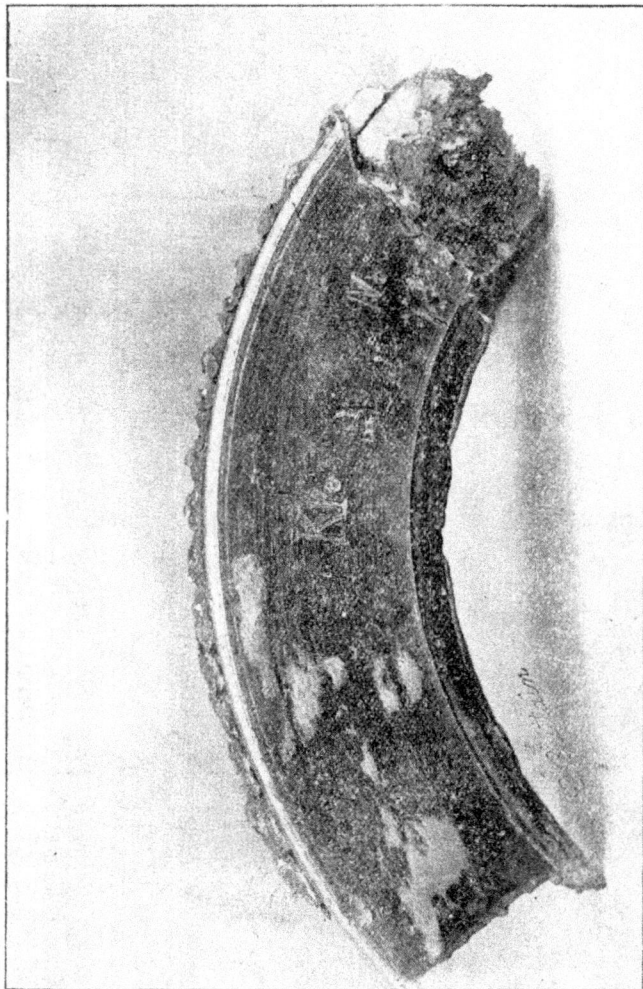

A piece of German "Kultur," West Hartlepool.

II.

EAST COAST ATTACKED.

Wake! For my Banner is at last unfurled
To flaunt its boastful message to the World:
  War to the Death! My Culture to enforce
With Challenge after Ultimatum hurled!
The Rubaiyat of William the War-Lord.

Why was the East coast attacked? Why should the
Hartlepools, Scarborough and Whitby be pounded with
German metal? Germany with her million-armed hosts to
dominate the land, with the second of the world's navies
to sweep the seas—surely these three towns, industrial and
sanatorial, could add but little, if any, to the glory of the
greatest people who ever sought to subdue the world by
force of arms. No, not even if they were reduced to ruins
and all their people slain! In one of our many fights with
France, Marshal de Conflans would not even permit his
gunners to use hollow or incendiary shells. They were
not, he said, generally used by polite nations, and the
French ought to fight according to the laws of honour.
Is not Germany, with civilising influences enough to
regenerate the world, a "polite" nation? After Louvain,
Vise, Termonde, Aerschot, after the Hartlepools, Scarborough
and Whitby, the world must make answer. Why, then,
was the East coast attacked? Such a question leads to the
larger one:—Why did Germany attack any one—Russia,
Belgium, France, England—at all? Leaving the devious
courses of European diplomacy, as it has spread its net
over a long number of years, diplomacy which has for its
beginning and end the pulling down of one nation and the
setting up of another, one must look for the direct causes
elsewhere. It is not enough to say that Britain staked
her all because of her treaty pledges to preserve the
neutrality of Belgium. That, no doubt, weighed heavily
with her, but it was impossible for this country, only
twenty-five miles from the other side of the English
Channel, to look on while France was reduced to a

15

German Protectorate. To do so would not only have left her naked to the tender mercies of the nation that aspires to be her greatest enemy, but would have strained her existence to the breaking-point. Her command of the sea would, sooner or later, have been openly challenged, the integrity of her shores would have been imperilled. It took our nation, as a whole, a long time to pierce the haze of German diplomacy, though it necessitated no powerful mental searchlight to do so. Those who were best versed in the wiles of the Teuton foresaw what was coming. "The Day" had long been set apart, the hour and the Man had been appointed. It is a good trait in our national character that we should be slow to suspect infamy in others. But the writing was all over the wall. It was plain for all who were not constitutionally precluded from seeing, that we had been weighed by the German and found wanting. He was fully equipped with every weapon, mental and material, to take over our business, to usurp our office, to thoroughly purge our Empire of all its deadly influences that had taken hold of it. The world had never yet produced so majestic a specimen of an imperial race, never one so morally endowed with all the christian virtues. And some of us really believed that it might be so. They said "Judge not, that ye be not judged." We must have respect for the opinions of others, and it is useless now to argue "what might have been." Yet nearly the whole of Belgium with much of Northern France has been flattened out, trodden under foot, centuries of noble work and honest toil ruthlessly destroyed. The abomination of desolation has overtaken it, four nations have copiously watered that unhappy soil with their blood. The fatalist will say "Such things must be. It is the expiation demanded of us when the predestined moment arrives." Others, with great force, will contend that had we spent a few millions a year, in view of the signs, knowing that the national toast of Germany was "To the Day!" we should have been spared sacrificing the fittest of our manhood, millions of our money every day. The Germans, themselves, admit it. Matured German philosophy had given us this:—

1. " War is a good thing in itself. All advance is founded upon struggle. Each nation has a right, indeed a duty, to use violence where its interests are concerned and there is tolerable hope of success."

2. " 'Love the brotherhood!' This law can claim no significance for the relations of one country to another, since its applications to politics would lead to a conflict of duties. It tells us to love our individual enemies, but does not remove the conception of enmity."

3. " Since almost every part of the globe is inhabited, new territory must, as a rule, be obtained at the cost of its possessors—that is to say, by conquest, which thus becomes the law of necessity."

4. Then the only course left is to acquire the necessary territory by war. Thus the instinct of self-preservation leads inevitably to war, and the conquest of foreign soil. It is not the possessor, but the victor, who then has the right."

5. " Arbitration treaties must be peculiarly detrimental to an aspiring people. An arbitration court can never replace in its effects and consequences a warlike decision."

6. " Under certain circumstances, it is not only the right but the moral and political duty of the statesman to bring about war."

7. " The Christian duty of sacrifice for something higher does not exist for the State."

8. " In one way or another we must square our account with France. France must be so completely crushed that she can never again come across our path."

9. " Conditions may arise which are more powerful than the most honourable intentions. The country's own interests must then turn the scale."

This is German as it is spoken to-day. But the Anglo-Saxon is a stubborn creature. Just as likely as not he might ask : " Who made thee a ruler and a judge over us? Wilt thou slay us as thou didst the Dane, the Austrian and the Frenchman yesterday, as thou art insiduously destroying the wretched, misguided Turk to-day?" And the German

would certainly answer back and say, " Yes, I will surely
rule over thee and judge thee, thou wicked. sinner, and
will slay thee and take thy belongings in the process."

It is comparatively easy for any one nation, with men
and money, to find a pretext for making war upon another.
Statesmen and diplomatists are often brewing trouble when
the ordinary man is accrediting them with the most pacific
intentions. Diplomacy is the firstborn of the father of lies.
In 1870, Bismarck forged or altered a telegram. The
French declared war as the result of his duplicity. In six
weeks France was overrun by the German hordes and Paris
soon on the way to " stew in its own juice."

The complete humiliation of France by the triumphal
entry of swaggering Junkerdom into its capital, the spoiling
of her territory by the grabbing of Alsace and Lorraine,
like that of Schleswig-Holstein, the attempt to cripple
France by levying an indemnity of 200 milliards—this, in
total, was the flood tide-mark, the highest altitude, the full
measure of Germany's power. Thereafter, she was to
morally and politically decay. Moltke, the subtle strategist,
was to go to his fathers, Bismarck, the unscrupulous, but
big-brained statesman, was hustled into seclusion. There
was no Napoleon, no Attila left, only Wilhelm II. Germany
was as drunk with pride of battle as she has been to-day
with the choice vintages of sunny France. The smell of
blood maddens the great beasts of prey. Denmark had
been pushed back, Austria shot down, France despoiled.
Germany, according to her professors, had cut a big sod
in the line that was to carry her in triumph round the
world.

> " How oft the sight of means to do ill deeds
> Makes ill deeds done ! "

Listen to Bernhardi :—

> " Even English attempts at *rapp ochement* must not
> blind us to the real situation. We may at most use
> them to delay the necessary and inevitable war until
> we may fairly imagine we have some prospect of
> success."

Treitschke wrote :—

> " Our last and greatest reckoning is to be with Great
> Britain."

Those dread days of 1870 were the salvation of France, as these dark ones of 1914-17 might well be for our own beloved country. Even that small affair on the North-East coast tried us in the furnace, tested the quality of the metal that was in us, proved to us the real uses of adversity, made us realise in one grim forty minutes what mighty issues were at stake as we never did before. For the message was plain. What was possible in a raid might, under favourable conditions, cover an invasion. Then the final reckoning would have come, " Der Tag " would have arrived.

> " We will never forego our hate.
> We have all but a single hate.
> We love as one, we hate as one,
> We have but one foe and one alone—
> ENGLAND."

Though France in the forty-four years that had elapsed since Sedan had regained her old positon in the counsels of Europe, had rallied her countrymen, recuperated in courage and strength, had indeed come away from her former self under the Empire, she was not ready when the long-overhanging cloud burst and the world-quake of the Great War shuddered the world. But she was cleaner in heart, more supple in limb.

Kaiser William showed his hand when he wrote his celebrated telegram to Kruger, but he was powerless for real mischief because the trident kept the seas. He must be as great by sea as he was by land. Britain drew closer to France. There are some who maintain even now that had we been free from European entanglements we should now have the satisfaction of merely sorrowing over other nations' misfortunes. But despite the neutrality of Belgium, to which we were pledged, we could never stand by and see France bled to death. To do so meant a conscript army, a more powerful fleet, a military and naval expenditure that might well have broken our backs. Germany tested the strength of this understanding or compact in 1906 and again in 1911. The overbearing, dictatorial attitude assumed by the Kaiser, as occasion prompts, is reflected in the upstart manner of many of his subjects who find a home, bed and board, in England. This "Lord of all I survey" manner runs in the blood of numbers of those who have prospered at our hands, fed at our tables, been honoured with distinctions in high places at home and abroad. "Prosperity doth best discover vice." This was apparent in 1906 when France, bullied by her one-time conqueror, took part in the conference at Algeciras. The Emperor desired to find a line of cleavage by which he might separate England and France. So, too, in 1911. He almost set Europe by the ears by the despatch of the Panther to Agadir. Bismarck's advice to his master was never to fight two great European Powers at the same time. But Wilhelm II. was a greater than Bismarck. He was of sterner stuff. If the State called, if war demanded, his subjects might be relied upon, if necessary, to regard as their greatest enemies the members of their own households. They were then to act accordingly, that is as they were told. On August 4, 1914, Wilhelm II. tried his third gamble. The integrity of his Empire, the position, the prosperity of his people was the stake. All Europe was to be a welter of blood.

Britain had given of her surplus population to her overseas dominions. Some of these possessions were won by conquest, some had been purchased, others had been made over to us by treaty. They, among other great gifts, were the dowry of our forefathers. We had inherited them. They were united to us by ties of blood. They spoke the same language. Their interests were ours. But Germany, now a great industrial people, could trade with them, as freely as ourselves. If any of them gave us a preference that was only because of the natural sympathy between a mother and her children. So far as we were concerned the seas of the world were open to all ships. Here, at home, was a free market for Germany the while she imposed a twenty per cent. tariff on our goods. Germany had acquired colonial settlements in East and South-West Africa, in the East Indian Archipelago, in the Pacific Ocean. But she had not the colonising instinct. Her feet were swift to shed blood. That contempt for everything which had not the hall-mark of her people made her despised. She wanted more air, certainly more light. But it was no

fault of ours if her population, by congestion, stepped
upon one another's toes. We could not help it if all the
habitable land of the globe were used up. Our colonies
had not implored us to give them a German overlord. If
Germany wanted elbow-room, the last way to get it was by
artillery fire, the bayonet point and the sword thrust.
In Disraeli's "Curiosities of Literature" is given, as an
example of the singularities of war, that the governors of
the Scythian provinces gave annually a feast to those who
had valiantly, with their own hands, despatched their
enemies. The skulls of the vanquished served for their
cups; and the quantity of wine they were allowed to drink
was proportioned to the number of skulls they possessed.
The youth, who could not yet boast of such martial
exploits, contemplated distantly the solemn feast, without
being permitted to approach it. This institution formed
courageous warriors. From the reports of the Belgian and
French Commissions of Inquiry we gather that the German
"valiants," who so chivalrously did to death their treaty
friends and bordering neighbours, placed no limit to the
number of their cups in the hour of their greatest victories.
And no doubt after their brilliant feat of arms in the
bombardment of three towns that were unable to hit back
many beer barrels were emptied. We know that the
Berlinese went giddy, lost all stately decorum, when they
learnt of the full extent of the damage done and of the
death and bodily injury dealt out. Life is a great gift.
Surely it is as sacred as honour. If war is among the
things inevitable, if men must fight, and progress most
along the lines of scientific destruction, nothing can justify
risking this precious gift but the defence of our hearths
and homes, that is our liberty, of right against might, of
justice against cruel wrong. Compared with the shell-fire
in the Allies' trenches that upon the East coast towns
was a mere pin-prick. But it was a measure of German
hate, perhaps of impotent rage. Many will see in it a
portent of ultimate defeat.

It is sorrowfully surprising that a vast body of our
countrymen should still be ignorant of the causes which
underlie the Great War, should have but little knowledge
of the fuse that fired the magazine and set the world

ablaze. And yet if we marshal every fact that can be brought to bear upon it the one reason which contains all others is that Germany was ready. "The Day" had arrived when her eagle, full-fledged, was to hover over and then swoop down upon old civilizations and new, impressing the imprint of its militant claw upon lion and lamb alike. The smaller States—Belgium, Holland, the rest of Denmark, with Switzerland, were to hear the beating of the great bird's wing en route. They were to be paralysed by fear and then stowed away in the cultured crop. For years lines were being laid down leading to these countries, railways that had no object and use other than for military purposes, strategic roads over which, when the hour was ripe and the Man had tuned up his courage, were to be hurried, with startling rapidity, the brutal instruments of war. Much has been written on all this, and much more will have to be written before a great mass of our people grasp the inmost truth that this conflict has issues which, to themselves, transcend all others. Are they willing to hand over their birthright for a mess of German pottage? Is this such a small matter that they can afford to stand idly by while blood is being poured out like water that their inheritance might not be taken by the burglar of Berlin? That forty minutes under shell-fire that we bore so bravely, that desolating scourge by which Scarborough was beaten, the desecration of the early Christian shrines of St. Hilda's and of Whitby Abbey effected—these, all, were but insignificant wounds to our national pride compared with the degradation, the wholesale murder that would follow upon a successful invasion of our shores. And if the enemy is not beaten back and shorn of his locks, he will put his hand to the pillars which sustain our Imperial home and pull them down. This chapter will not be written in vain if, in however small measure, it aid some of us to see more clearly the things that matter, the issues that are to determine our right to live as freeborn men, as citizens of no mean State. If we grasp all this we shall go on from strength to strength; Kitchener will only ask for more men to get them; the "silver bullet" of the Allies will determine the final account. Were Germany asked for the root cause of her bitter feelings towards us, what answer could she make?

A few unconsidered trifles, which refused to explode.

Hunter Street, West Hartlepool:
(Back premises of Donald Brown & Co.)
(See page 129)

For many years we had looked upon this enterprising and prosperous people, next to our cousins in America, as our best friends, our nearest allies. We had stood by them, in days long ago, on many a hard fought field. Perhaps to our shame, certainly to our hurt, we had given to many of their professors and men of science preference over our own countrymen in our Indian Empire and the colonies. London and our large towns found employment for thousands of German emigrants. These, numbers of them, intermarried with our race, though, as we see now, often for the base purpose of securing an intermediary who should betray the trust reposed in them. German science has shown great aptitude in developing the ideas, improving upon the discoveries of others. Through our indolence and stupidity this has cost us dear in the markets of the world. We grumbled when the cheaper goods made in Germany pushed our own from the shop shelves. But we went on in our easy-going way, always anxious to avoid strife. To put off the evil day which so many of our experienced men saw was coming, our statesmen almost humiliated themselves to strike a bargain on our joint expenditure in the building of fleets. This was construed as weakness, as decadence, if not as a lack of courage. Germany was too puffed up with martial pride, in her own estimation such a prodigy in moral, military and material strength, as to pour contempt on our efforts for peace. She was too far moved by envy, hatred and malice and all uncharitableness to see any good in us. We stood in the way of her seizing the unlawful heritage she had marked and mapped out for her own by right of place as the foremost nation of all time. Knowing what we do now of German methods of warfare in France, Russia and Belgium, our resentment has deepened at the thought of the accusations brought against our troops during the Boer War. Under long-continued provocation we did not attempt to smash the German Fleet, as we should have done in Nelson's time, but we looked for friends on the continent of Europe who could see the trouble that was coming and who might act with us when the plot of the enemy was ripe.

A war which would shake mankind in the " four corners of the world " was inevitable. It were a vain hope to cry peace when the central Power in Europe was determined to break the peace the moment the opportunity offered. "A thing that is wholly a sham cannot endure for ever; its doom is certain." That was a German professor's allusion to our Empire. The world has already formed its opinion of which is the sham empire; the jackboots of Prussia have no reliable friends in the Old World or the New. Dr. E. J. Dillon in the Daily Telegraph of January 14, 1915, narrates an amusing incident, showing how Turkish flight was checked in Caucasia by a Cossack expedient. He says:—

> "An amusing instance of Russian ingenuity is reported by the *Temps* from Petrograd. It appears that, having taken over 7,000 prisoners at Sarykamysch and Ardahan, the Russian commander had not a sufficient escort to convey them to the interior, whereupon the Cossack guards cut the buttons off the prisoners' trousers, and thus compelled the Turks to employ their hands in the cause of decency and comfort during the long march and to abandon thoughts of flight."

The moral support of any worthy nation to another at war is a commanding asset. The Junker sham has cut off all that was likely to brace it up in its march to victory and to glory by its pretensions, by the primitive savagery with which it has conducted this war. The East coast raid was typical of its other methods. In Bismarck's words "It was not worth the bones of a Pomeranian grenadier." It certainly brought "frightfulness" with it, but at the same time it assured the condemnation of every knightly soldier, every chivalrous people.

As we have seen, the German statesmen and strategists who mattered, the men who now rested from their labours of 1870, saw the danger to their country if engaged at the same moment on two fronts, against France on the one side and Russia on the other. But Kaiserdom, the new moulder of German destiny, had no such scruples. All was ready. The army had been increased, the guns multiplied beyond precedent, the navy annually strengthened; indeed Wilhelm II. had already announced himself to the world as "The Admiral of the Atlantic." The one thing needful was to keep Great Britain out of the bloody

enterprise. Her hour would come afterwards. The chariot
of Russia was slow to move; the war with Japan had been
its undoing. Even should Italy decline to take part in
an aggressive war, Austria could hold unprepared Russia
in check while France was overrun, Paris taken, a war
indemnity fixed, the Channel coast seized and held in an
unrelenting grip. Then the infatuated locust-legions could
turn round upon Russia and eat up her land.

Britain's hand was stayed. She was riven by political
faction; the two Irelands had sharpened their swords; the
dread of civil war was over the land; India and Egypt were
seditiously unsteady. The informer, above stairs and below,
assured all and sundry in Germany that Britain would not,
could not fight. Only a pretext was necessary. Unlike
the arguments at Algerciras and Agadir the one proposed
now was to be clinched. Austria was the dupe, Germany
the doper. Austria was to make the running, for Germany
to beat the time record. The pretext was found in the
murder of an Austrian prince and princess by Serbian
regicides. Bosnia and Herzegovina had virtually become
Austrian territory when Russia was weak through her war
with Japan. Russia remonstrated, but Germany humiliated
the northern Power by a diplomatic " Hands off! " Austria
determined to make the murder an excuse for further
inroads upon the Balkans. Russia would not swallow this
further insult, this challenge to her pride.

All the intrigue which led up to this impasse was mere
by-play. The German poison was ready; those who refused
the drug must have it forced down their throats. It was
useless for a Liberal Government to strain patience to
breaking point, to try here, to try there for some way
out of the web so cunningly woven. " The Day " had
arrived, the hour had almost struck, Germany was in
ambush for the pounce. Russia felt the edge of her sword
and thought that with a few more turns upon the whetstone
of fate it was ready for its work. But, as we know now,
there was treachery in high places. Germany, backed up
her Austrian ally, threw down the gauntlet, and when
Belgian neutrality was violated Great Britain leaped into
the arena, to take part in a struggle brought about by
Germany to depose her ultimately from her proud position
among the nations.

III.

HARTLEPOOL, PAST AND PRESENT.

The meteor flag of England
Shall yet terrific burn;
Till danger's troubled night depart,
The star of peace return.
—*Ye Mariners of England.*

By great, good fortune, only some hundred thousand, out
of the forty-five millions of people who live in these
islands, were liable to the destructive fire of the finest and
fleetest of Germany's brand new navy. Berlin has its
banners ready, its brass tuned to the "Watch on the
Rhine," whenever its Emperor, truthful, lying or obscure,
tells of victory in the Great War to his smell-feast people.
We have no such undying hatred for them as they boast
to have for us, though much time will have winged its
flight before we and our allies forget their murderous
onslaught on the peace of Europe. And if we remind
them of the littleness of their greatness in making this
attack upon, at least three defenceless towns, it will not
be to further arouse their dislike of us, their too simple-
minded neighbours. We have forgiven and forgotten much;
we should have endured much more cajolery and deceit
before making aggressive war against them. Indeed it is
almost impossible to think of this nation being provoked
into an attack upon Germany save when its own territory
was at stake. But that would have been a defensive war.
So is this in which we are engaged. Said the German:
"In one way or another we must square our account with
France. France must be so completely crushed that she
can never again come across our path." This that follows
is much more illuminating for ourselves:—

"A pacific agreement with England is a will-o'-the-wisp,
which no serious German statesman would trouble to
follow. We must always keep the possibility of war
with England before our eyes and arrange our political

28

and military plans accordingly. We need not concern
ourselves with any pacific protestations of English
politicians, publicists, and Utopians, which cannot alter
the real basis of affairs."

Though Germany was disappointed at our taking a hand
in the terrible game of war she had fostered, prepared for,
and manœuvred into being, yet the statesmen of both our
great political Parties were not slow to see that it involved
our lives, our homes, the liberty we are so proud to possess.
Putting the Hartlepools under shell-fire was no great feat
of arms for the second navy of the world. Of its own
choosing, it was really its baptism of fire, but only from
gallant little batteries that it knew could not seriously
damage it. Otherwise it would not have come. Nelson at
Trafalgar, the Japanese at Port Arthur certainly did
greater, braver things than this.

Many who read these pages will know of the bombardment,
though perhaps little of the two towns, Hartlepool and
West Hartlepool. In truth, most of those who live any
distance away from them will have regarded them as one
and the same place—Hartlepool. But they are two distinct
towns with defined boundaries, each under separate
administrative powers. One is old, the other young; if we
may, one is mother, the other an only son. Hartlepool,
with its venerable shrine of St. Hilda's, carries us back
to Saxon and Norman times. Its list of Mayors tells of
its long civic life. Near as it was to the lands of the
Picts and Scots, in the fighting line of the advancing
marauding Danes after they had crossed the North Sea,
it must often have felt the shock of savage battle, though
not more savage than that waged by more " kultured "
people now. Were its full history recorded we should
hear of pirates landing near its rocky coast, of savage
border warfare in which it took part, of jousts and tourna-
ments and martial arrays among the belted knights of the
Middle Ages. Proud of its antiquity, it still struggles
on in a world of new things, striving to keep its head
above the attacks of time. Its face to the sea was, down
to late years, guarded by huge masses of limestone rock,
but only the foundations of these can now be seen at

receding tide. The all-devouring waves have swept the
figured cliffs away. A wall of granite and concrete,
providing a delightful promenade, has taken their place,
evidence once again of man's attempted mastery over
nature.

In our own day, among all the changing scenes which
have illustrated the pages of its varied career, it has
looked up to see fleets of airships scudding before the
breeze, circling round and sliding down on the back of
the air, to race to a standstill on the neighbouring sands.
Zeppelins, too, with their torpedoes of the air, have hovered
near it or over it in search of our unwearied Fleet.
Destroyers, submarines, torpedo-boats are continually
moving, or lying at anchor in its harbour, waiting and
watching for the implacable foe should he attempt to
imprint his swaggering heel upon the soil of freedom.
Portions of the old wall which once formed its protective
rampart are still standing. That wall was in its entirety
when the proud Armada of Spain met Drake and Frobisher
and Hawkins in the English Channel during the days of
good Queen Bess. It was there as the Dutch sailed up
Thames and Medway when Charles II. was trying his hand
at kingship. Quite likely it heard the sound of the guns
on one or more of the many occasions when the French
under Napoleon attempted to find footing on our soil.
But never till December 16, 1914, did it receive, as an
early morning reminder, a full blast of modern shell.
Though bruised and broken by an overpowering fire, it
answered bravely back and came undaunted out of the trial.

Naturally, the old wall, the promenade, with its lighthouse
and Heugh batteries and extended shore-line beyond, would,
one and all, be dangerous vantage-ground when battleships
were punching holes in England's sides or in the walls
of her homesteads beyond. But in summer and early
autumn, when the sun nets the waves with gold, or at
night, when the lights splash them with pallor, these are
pleasant spots. For those who prefer the greater glory,
the unconquerable might of the sea, the moor behind will
enable them to see the frothy spume leap up, overflow
and fall back in all its tempestuous grandeur. The air
too, has a grip in it which should rouse the blood of the

enervated and depressed, as effectively as the breezes from the mountain slopes of Alps or Pyrenees. The Hartlepools are healthy, the people long-lived, the summer heat moderated by the winds that blow in from the sea, the winters comparatively mild. If they do not possess the luxurious trivialities of the recognized seaside watering-places, there is much in them both to interest and enjoy.

It is a strange sight for Britons of this generation to see their coasts scarred and broken by lines of entrench-ments, the parapets covered with sandbags, the landing-places bristling with wire-entanglements. The enemy is at the gate. It is hard for those who know nothing of the brutal realities of war to realise that invasion, if foolishly rash, is yet possible. Not since the days of Napoleon have these island shores been menaced and harassed by a hostile foe. It seems impossible for us to be roused into the belief that airships are nightly threatening us with their bombs, that submarines are burrowing through our narrow waters to make our ships their prey, that squadrons should cross the North Sea at night, distract us with their boom and rattle, and scuttle off home again, fearful of their skins, in the early morning. This is decidedly a new national experience. But we, chastened in our insular pride, shall weather the storm. "Freedom shrieked when Kosciusko fell." Freedom would perish for a while were Prussian militarism to hold sway and treachery triumph. The world will not submit, though legions of devils have to be cast out.

Hartlepool is an old fishing-town. Its boats drift, trawl and long-line. You may see the salmon and herring nets drying on the pebbly beach. The new fish quay presents a wondrous sight after a great catch. The rail runs alongside the quay. The ice boats sling aloft their frozen blocks. Scotch girls come when the herrings shoal. Then, cleaning, smoking, and curing engage these willing hands.

Most of our principal seats of manufacturing industry lie upon, or near to, our coal-fields. To our central position among the great land-masses of the globe, to our natural stores of coal and iron, we owe much. The Hartlepools are in touch with the rich seams of coal of the second largest of our coal-fields as these eastward seams dip away under the sea from their outcrop further west. Royalties cease when the miner has driven his main a certain distance seaward from the shore. The development of this extreme fringe of mineral wealth has largely increased the export of coal from the two ports. The sinking of shafts through a thick cap of magnesian limestone, and downwards through quicksands largely charged with water, has been costly and difficult, but by novel means, such as freezing the water-logged sand, these obstacles have been overcome. The output of fuel-wealth promises to be very large. To the stranger it is a new experience to watch men, women and children raking up coal in heaps to drain on the seashore. This is a harvest of the sea for the poor. The intermittent supply seems to depend upon certain winds and tidal currents, and to be due to the wear and tear of outcropping seams at the bed of the sea. The marvel is that the store of this coal-sand, from whatever natural processes continually at work, should appear inexhaustible.

The "Hartlepools' Woods," as they have been facetiously called, stretch for a long distance along the sidings of the N.E. Railway. They are no longer, however, the evergreen and deciduous trees of the forest, but far-stretching piles of sawn timber and pine trunks of various lengths and sizes—mining timber for propping up the threatening roofs, as the coal miner pursues his dangerous task. The port is one of our largest centres for the import of timber, principally from the Baltic and White Seas. The huge accumulation of wood did not provide a great fire, as the German raiders probably expected it would, when under the more or less indiscriminate shelling to which both towns were subjected.

Industrial Hartlepool, some 21,000 people, finds other outlets for its energies in shipbuilding, marine engine and electrical plant making. Its harbour, protected from north-east storms by a massive breakwater, leads to spacious docks. These landlocked havens for the ships that go outward and return have, during the last few years, been opened out and their quay facilities extended and improved. The two towns are linked up by rail and tramway. The N.E.R. holds a monopoly in railway transport, but provides

Sandwell Watergate : part of the old Walls of Hartlepool.

(See page 129)

The first shell struck this house and killed the two Misses Kay.
(See page 90)

an excellent train service through Newcastle to northern Britain and by York, to London and the South. Hartlepool has its Carnegie Library, and is, educationally, well equipped by its "Henry Smith" and Council Schools. It is justly proud of its hospital, which occupies part of the site of a Greyfriars Monastery founded in 1258 by Robert de Bruce. This institution was the place of mercy and of refuge for the toll of maimed and wounded in the German aimless attack. In common with the Cameron Hospital and other hastily improvised buildings, it was the recipient of warm commendation from those in high authority for its readiness, its tender handling and skilful treatment of the large number of innocent stricken ones suddenly given to its charge.

With the sporting proclivities of the northern counties the stranger to them will soon be made acquainted.

"A clear fire, a clean hearth, and the rigour of the game."

Hartlepool is a home of Rugby football and has carried off, year after year, all the possible local honours of that strenuous game. Golf is provided for by an 18-hole course laid out by the Hartlepool Golf Club on the sea banks and among the sand dunes to the north of the town. The distinctive features of this defended port, whose history carries one back to the Crusades and beyond, are :—

(1) St. Hilda's Parish Church, with Norman porch and buttressed tower, dating back, through all its beginnings, to the earliest chapters of our national history.

(2) The Breakwater (440 yards) protecting the harbours.

(3) The Promenade, facing a wide, open sea, with Teesmouth and the Yorkshire cliffs to the south-east.

(4) The Fish Quay of recent date, with great capacity.

(5) The Lighthouse, built in 1847.

(6) The Docks, with their shipping and appliances for the handling of coal and timber.

(7) The Shipyards and Engine Works.

Hartlepool was made a borough by King John in 1200. The Corporation Seal dates back to the thirteenth century, and has on one side a representation of a hart in a pool with a hound at its heels, and on the other a figure of St. Hilda between two priests.

WEST HARTLEPOOL: ITS RISE AND PROGRESS.

West Hartlepool may be called a modern industrial town of seventy years growth and 70,000 people. The harbour and dock, to which it owes its parentage, was opened in 1847. What Hartlepool could no longer do by virtue of age and weariness of the flesh, the scion of the " Old House " was called upon to make good. Wedged in, as it is, between the ironstone of the Clevelands and the coal of seaward Durham, with a broad sea in front, continental markets in the distance, and an open country at its back, it has natural possessions and advantages which should ensure it continued prosperity. On its flank, only three miles distant to the south, is the broad estuary of the Tees. Towns that are lame and halt are not, to a vigorous community, of such value as family groups of a like persuasion and purpose. They are the comrades who, strong in wind and limb, make the pace or whip up the flagging. West Hartlepool is fortunate in its connections, and perhaps like some nations, in having no history to sprag its wheels by sentimental precedent. By road, river, sea and rail, it is linked up with the prosperous communities living at Newcastle and Sunderland on the north, with Middlesbrough, Stockton and Darlington on the river banks of the Tees to the south. The reclaimed land at the mouth of this river calls to it for a speeding up of those activities already begun.

> " To have done is to hang quite out of fashion,
>   Like a rusty mail in monumental mockery."

West Hartlepool has not done; her greater opportunities are just beginning. With youth and vigour in her being she has all the incentives which should move the enterprising to greatly prosper. She has had the fire of the guns to stimulate her ardour, to arouse her fighting spirit. Life is a series of experiences, some of which we like to

remember, most of them we would fain forget. To be
under shell fire is not one of the pleasantest of these.
Some things, some men, are put to base uses, but all have
their roll-call as the hour strikes, as the centuries move
on. All are not equipped for scattering deeds of kindness.
Some, indeed, like the Prussian giant, distribute, with a
large hand, their own distinctive tokens of love.

The two 'Pools join hands across the sea by the ferry-
boats of the old harbour. The ferrymen kept bravely to
their work as the shells in their fall drove the people from
the danger zone. The Parliamentary Borough and Port
of the Hartlepools includes the Borough of Hartlepool and
the County Borough of West Hartlepool. The mother
church—the Parish Church of Stranton—dates back to
Norman times. It occupies a central position on the site
of the old village, relics of which may still be seen, but
the greater number of which have fallen prey to the builder
of more modern houses. Old Stranton is now nearly lost
in the new. The road from Stockton is the highway through
it. At its junction with Church square a broader thorough-
fare leads eastwards, by Church Street, to the docks and
ferry. The Stockton Road is continued to Hartlepool and,
by a branch road at the Cemetery, to Hart, and so on
to Sunderland. Built on the gentlest of slopes, West
Hartlepool unfits the muscles for climbing giddy heights,
just as its invigorating air makes, to a long resident, a
softer, warmer climate less agreeable.

It is on this slope, stretching westwards from the sand-
dunes that once, hereabouts, confronted the sea, that the
younger Hartlepool saw the beginnings of a bustling life.
As it matured, it pushed out its arms north and south.
The new collieries will bring it into touch with a large
mining population, and industrial activity, taking root on
the north bank of the Tees estuary, will make enterprise
and development near neighbours.

Two memorial statues, facing east and west, do honour
to Ralph Ward-Jackson and Sir William Gray. Between
them, in Church Square, stands the shrine of Christ Church,
conspicuous by its favoured position and its architectural
design. Doubtless the creative foresight of more than one
man led to the foundation of West Hartlepool being laid,

but to Ralph Ward-Jackson the new docks, the fount and
source of all that followed, the port is believed to be indebted.
That seems consistent with the fact that money raised as
a testimonial of gratitude to him was, on his untimely death,
spent in the purchase of land, now planted and watered as
a small, yet beautiful park, bearing his name. In more
recent years the banks of a stream which more than once
submerged the streets of Stranton with flood water, were
purchased by the Corporation as an open space for the
growing, industrial part of the community in its vicinity.
This is now known as the Burn Valley Gardens. In both
recreation grounds are beautiful bowling-greens, and to
the west of the park is the new cricket ground happy in
most pleasant surroundings. Ralph Ward-Jackson could
hardly have anticipated the time when Sir William Gray
would, more than once, carry off the blue riband for
building and launching the highest total tonnage in the
shipbuilding trade, nor could either of them have ever
dreamt of a day when the town, both of them did so much
to develop, should be shot at by marksmen of the
German High Seas Fleet. Nor could Mr. William Cresswell
Gray (now Sir William Cresswell Gray, Bart.), who
succeeded to his father's large enterprises, have entertained the probability of the commodious baths, he
generously gave to the town, being almost immediately
after their completion used for a garrison military force
defending our seaward line in the time of Britain's
greatest war. In these closing days of January, 1915,
West Hartlepool is full of brave men preparing to take
their part in a conflict which keeps the world awake in a
nightmare of anticipation and alarm. The forces of
destruction have been let loose; the fate of nations is in
the balance; Eastern and Western Europe are seeking to
join hands in an endeavour to crush between them a last
effort of feudal power.   .

The streets of West Hartlepool are laid out in rectangular
lines. In them are excellent shops replete with goods of
every kind. Happily, the chief business centres did not
greatly suffer from German violence. The madness of
the few did not seriously disturb the equanimity of the
many. Tramways connect up east and west, north and

south. Gas and electricity light up the streets. The water supply is abundant, the death-rate remarkably low. Splendid schools, technical, higher grade and elementary, have been built. The Public Library and Athenæum have comfortable reading-rooms. The Cameron Hospital, on higher ground, is a real home for the sick. Never were its resources more severely tried, though not found wanting, than in the hour of the great emergency.

The many industries of the port provide employment for the bulk of the population. Work is found at the shipbuilding yards, at the docks, at the iron and steel works, in the engine and boiler works, at the paper mills, at the metal expansion works, and at a multitude of various subsidiary factories and trades. The import of timber, the export of coal, means commercial relations with all parts of the world, work, too, in busy times for many able and willing hands.

Actuated by a desire to secure more open spaces as playgrounds for the increasing population, the Corporation, by a spirited policy, acquired the sea banks, which front the bay from Newburn Bridge to the little suburb of Seaton Carew. These banks for a distance of more than a mile have been levelled, improved and provided with shelters. On them has been erected the sea baths to which allusion has been made. Entrenchments in the sandy soil of this coast-strip, with sentinels on watch and a garrison ready for an emergency-call, are evidences that here, as elsewhere, the East coast has anticipated the coming of the foe.

> " Yea, I am old,
> But this thing they forget:
> Whate'er I hold,
> Where'er my foot be set,
> Under whatever sky my Flag be flung,
> Freedom is in its folds to keep men young."

Shallow water, free from strong currents, off these banks, makes bathing safe. Whether it would favour the landing of an enemy's troops is for others to decide. But we know to our hurt that battleships have come, perhaps to spy out this particular spot for future hostile reference. The

walk by the sea from the railway bridge towards the golf
links is made easy and pleasant by a broad tar macadam
footway. This was completed by Mr. Nelson F. Dennis,
the Borough Engineer, and has proved an attractive and
pleasant promenade. It faces a broad, open expanse of
the sea, having bold Yorkshire cliffs curving round to
Whitby and Scarborough on the south-east, with the old
wall of Hartlepool, breakwater and lighthouse on the
Heugh promontory, some two miles to the north. The
Cleveland Hills, the "iron-ore origin" of Middlesbrough
further up the Tees, form a noble flank of high ground
on the Yorkshire side of the river, at the mouth of which
is a breakwater, lighthouse and fort. This latter place of arms
is garrisoned by a Territorial force of the Durham Royal
Garrison Artillery which, with the Durham County Battalion,
showed such admirable coolness and grit as the enemy spit
fire and venomed shell on the morning of their hasty visit.
From the promenade walk may be seen merchantmen
passing to and fro in the offing, or the trawlers and cobles
entering or leaving the harbour mouth. Likely enough,
on the sandy slope below the walk, women and children
will be gathering and carrying away the coal which the
tide has cast up. At the moment, searchlights from the
Teesmouth battery direct, with fierce, suspicious eyes,
their expanding beams over sea, river and sky. The blast-
furnaces behind and those on the far side of the river add
their lurid glare, toned down by the modest, twinkling
lamps of Redcar Pier, or the more pretentious signal-lights
that herald the approach to the West Hartlepool railway
station.

Seaton Carew, like Old Stranton, has a long history.
Rail, tramway and promenade lead directly to it. Soon a
new road will connect it, by way of the river, with Middlesbrough. This will shorten the distance for vehicular and
foot traffic for towns north and south of the river and,
quite possibly, make Seaton Carew a place of rest-cure,
much more important than it is now, for the tired hands
and brains on either side of it. This little watering-place
has much to recommend it in its bracing air, its far-
stretching sands, its links, its fine, open sea.

West Hartlepool, like Hartlepool, has become quite a "show" place since the bombardment. Those who come to see its wounds should find relief in a survey of its still sound parts and pleasanter prospects:—

> The Council Chamber of the Municipal Buildings contains life-size portraits of pioneers, mayors, and enterprising citizens.
>
> The Ward-Jackson Park, with a tribute to heroes of the Boer War, is an imitation of no other.
>
> The making of ingots of steel and plating for ships should be seen after nightfall.
>
> A walk to Teesmouth by the sea banks will be found interesting and appetising.
>
> The Central Marine Engine Works and Richardson, Westgarth, & Co's. Engineering Works will interest the scientific and mechanical.
>
> The Docks during the full flood of timber importation are scenes of congested activity.

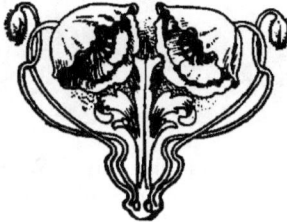

SCARBOROUGH.

Hartlepool has its St. Hilda's, Scarborough its Castle, Whitby its Abbey. These are treasures which appeal to a people who can look back upon the changing scenes of a long historic past. The deeds of nearly nine hundred years have been marshalled upon the calendars of those centuries since these islands were last invaded and laid under the heel of the conqueror. The beginnings of St. Hilda's were the very beginnings of Christianity. Scarborough's Castle was a feudal bulwark during the Wars of the Roses and the Civil War. The Abbey of Whitby is a venerable ruin of splendid Gothic art, sacred to the young and old of Britain as once a mother shrine for the offerings of an infant people. The German would seem to be possessed of a brain, half of which is of fine texture, the other half coarse and grossly barbarian. The savage in him has not been cast out; indeed it is master of the individual head and of all the parts owing it subjection. So the young barbarian at play battered at the roof of St. Hilda's, partly dismantled the remains of Scarborough Castle, and did not hestitate to add ruin to the

GERMAN RAID DEC. 16TH 1914 — SHELLS EXPLODING ON THE CASTLE WALLS, SCARBOROUGH.

(See page 43)

GERMAN RAID, DEC. 16TH, 1914. THE OLD BARRACKS, CASTLE HILL, SCARBOROUGH.

(See page 46)

ruins of Whitby Abbey. There was no gun to defend castle or abbey because, said the barbarian, the gunners had run away! The port of Hartlepool is for the industrially active; Scarborough for those who seek recreation in activity; Whitby favours the society of those who claim the seclusion of rest. The port was busy with rivet and with plate when the raider came. Scarborough and Whitby, hit hard by the war, were looking forward to the Christmas season to recoup and replenish. War makes the greatest demands only to effect the greatest losses.

Scarborough is so well known, so generally visited, as to need little pen description. The Yorkshire coast, from the mouth of the Tees to Flamborough Head, is chiselled with nature's finest sculpture. Beautiful valleys slope inland from it to the sterner moorland uplands. Scarborough has a glorious bay, a supple sand, attractions by cliff and hollow for resident and visitor alike.

What red flag did Scarborough flaunt to provoke the hostile action of the raiders? What had sunny Scarborough done to lash the German into such frenzy of passion? Where was the fort, where the gunners? All-the-year-bathers were taking their usual dip. Naked and unashamed, surely they were not fit sport for Imperial guns! True, a postman on his rounds was killed, but then he was attached to an intelligence department. In a milkman's horse was interned three pounds of Krupp's shell-mixture. Perhaps it was thought the poor, dumb creature would have been better employed in the furniture-removal business away in France and Belgium. The lighthouse was practically shot away, but, then, men love the dark, whose deeds are evil. Scarborough, like the 'Pools, was, more than half of it, in the dumb forgetfulness of a December sleep. That might have aroused the animosity of a very wide-awake people. The Castle wall was pierced, the Castle damaged, but these were relics of barbarism, and in traces of barbarism the Germans would allow nothing to rival them. The battery above the Marine Drive had been removed years ago. The only bit of artillery left was a 64-pounder prize-gun, such as may be seen in many of our public parks. It was Russian, and probably captured at Sebastopol, or in one of the battles of the Crimean War. Here, certainly, was some slight cause of provocation. It brought echoes from the battlefields of Poland.

But, putting all together, there was none but a German reason why the thunder of the guns and wail of 500 shells should for nearly twenty minutes have shaken and alarmed Scarborough as if it were a stronghold, a place of arms in a hated empire. And, saddest of all, nineteen unarmed civilians were killed and eighty wounded. As, elsewhere, many have since died, and many will yet die, from nervous shock received that morning. Yorkshire people are, however, proverbially stolid and stout-hearted under strain and stress of circumstances. Dennis and Sons, Ltd., in their London and Scarborough "Dainty" Series, tell us of an old woman whose house was pierced by a shell. "Yes, it's a pity," said she, "but I wouldn't have minded so much if I hadn't been doing my bit of cleaning." Another, asked to go downstairs for greater safety, replied, "I'll no go doonstairs, if the Lord wants me to be kilt, He'll see to it any road." And a third, on being told that the Germans were bombarding the town, said, "Hey! is it only guns? I was frightened it was thunder."

Scarborough was raided by two ships of the powerful squadron that came over on the night of December 15, 1914, from the German naval base about the mouth of the Elbe. Germans had, of course, visited this "Brighton of the North" before, but on pleasure, perhaps on business, bent. Like the crew of the German cruiser, so lavishly entertained by the trustful people of Dundee, the German visitors climbed the Castle cliff, looked across the wide expanse of the North Sea, admired, perhaps wondered, while all the time being trusted and fêted as guests. The new wounds added to the old scars of the Castle can but enhance its historic record. The "Red Cross," flying above the two large hospitals of Hartlepool and West Hartlepool, apparently gave the Germans pause in their most savage moments. Not so at Scarborough. The hospital, there, was struck. The patients cheerfully made way when the last salvo was fired and the wounded from house and street were being brought in. The old barracks on Castle Hill, used as a store, were mercilessly pounded. So were the Grand Restaurant, the Grand and Royal Hotels, so well known to the thousands who appreciate the charms of the town and neighbourhood. The Scarborough residence of the borough member (W. R. Rea, Esq.) was much damaged. Mr. Rea urged the Government to indemnify the owners of property in the three towns attacked for the loss they had sustained. Their claims were recognised.

Disappointed at Yarmouth by the shells falling short, the attacking flotilla, evidently piloted by one who knew every landmark and fathom, came within 600 yards of the shore. As the shells fired were for the most part 5.9 inch or 4 inch, it probably included the battle-cruiser, Seydlitz, and the protected cruiser, Graudenz. These two, with smaller vessels for mine-laying, afterwards steamed north to Whitby. The firing seems to have been even more reckless than at Hartlepool, and much private property was damaged. The wireless station, the gasworks and waterworks received the enemy's more fixed attention, but were only slightly injured. Naturally, as at the Hartle-pools, there was great alarm. At both places a great dread of being crushed by falling masonry led numbers of the inhabitants to rush into the streets, to make for the railway station or the open country. This was rash. It led to a greater death-roll than would otherwise have been the case. But the terror caused by the continuous roar and rattle of the broadsides was great. These people were ignorant of what was most prudent to do should such a terrifying experience overtake them. The majority were ignorant of the death-dealing effects of scattering, exploding shell. How were they to know? Even our brave troops have had to learn by experience how best to burrow out of danger. Many people in the towns attacked have since dug themselves in. They have provided places of refuge should the German Navy again indulge in this petty kind of warfare, utterly unworthy of the glorious traditions of the sea, contemptible from the first military and second naval power in the world. But this triumph of "frightful-ness" is not likely to be repeated. The lesson given by Admiral Beatty to the third raiding squadron on Sunday, January 24, 1915, will not readily be forgotten.

The following fatal cases, among all the sad ones, may be enumerated :—

No. 2, Wykeham Street has been called " the house of tragedy." Seven people were living in it on the morning of the bombardment. One of the last shells fired killed four of the inmates—Mrs. Bennett, a soldier son and two other children. Mr. Bennett and the other son were severely wounded.

At a corner of South Street two men were killed— Harry Frith, a driver, and Leonard Ellis, a porter.

Alfred Beale, a postman, was about to deliver letters at "Dunollie," when a shell burst in front of this residence and killed him, together with a maidservant in the library.

Mrs. G. H. Merryweather, of Prospect Road, was bringing friends to take refuge in her shop cellar, when a shell hit the building, and so severely wounded her that she died immediately afterwards.

A young woman picked up a crying baby. She had carried it to a bedroom, when a shell burst through the roof and killed both of them.

A servant went upstairs to assure her mistress that only gun-practising in the bay was the cause of the violent explosions. Following a great crash a few minutes later, the servant was killed, struck in the breast by a fragment.

The Castle Walls are ten feet thick. They were pierced in several places, and the old beacon was blown away. The Grand Hotel was hit by no less than thirty shells, and, damage done to it to the extent of more than £10,000. A 100-lb. shell entered the old men's bedroom in the Albert Hall of the Workhouse Buildings. It then passed through the dining room on the first floor and buried itself in the clay. Without the nose, it measured 22 inches in length, 6 inches in diameter, and weighed 83 lbs. During the early communion service at St. Martin's, the church was struck by three shells, but Archdeacon Mackarness went on with the service, quietly remarking that safety was as sure in the church as anywhere else.

Scarborough's loss by the flight of many of her residents and visitors must be heavy. She has, however, so many great natural advantages and attractions that, before the last day of the world-strife is over, she will have recovered her strength and hastened to add to her popularity.

The following list includes all those who have already died from the effects of the shell-fire to which they were subjected :—

SCARBOROUGH.

Mr. Alfred Beal, 50, Raleigh Street ...	41
Mrs. Johanna Bennett, 2, Wykeham Street	58
Mr. Alfred F. Bennett, 2, Wykeham Street	22
George James Barnes, 2, Wykeham Street	5
Miss Margaret Briggs, "Dunollie," Filey Road	30
Miss Edith Crosby, 1, Belvedere Road	39
Miss Ada Crowe, 124, Falsgrave Road	28
Mrs. Alice Duffield, 38, Esplanade	56
Mr. Leonard Ellis, 29, Londesborough Road	47
Mr. Harry Frith, 1, Bedford Street...	45
George Harland Taylor, North Street	15
Mr. Henry Harland, 8, Belle Vue Street	30
Mr. John Hall, J.P., C.C., 28, Westbourne Park...	65
Mrs. Emily Lois Merryweather, 43, Prospect Road	30
Miss Bertha McIntyre, 22, Westbourne Park	42
Mrs. Mary Prew, 17, Belle Vue Street ...	65
John Shield Ryalls, 22, Westbourne Park ...	14 months
John Christopher Ward, 2, Wykeham Street	10

WHITBY.

If Scarborough may be likened to a big, bouncing maid, ruddy and round, making Germany jealous, then matured Whitby, with its grey, wrinkled Abbey, would seem to have made her warriors ashamed in their treacherous, unresisted attack. The bombardment of the quaint, old fishing port began soon after nine in the morning, and was continued only for a few minutes. It was time for the Germans to turn tail and seek the protecting arms of the Vaterland. An effective British patrol squadron would doubtless by this time be apprised of their whereabouts, and would be rushing through the water in high glee at the chance of intercepting them. We know now that such an opportunity offered. The enemy ships were sighted, but pushing their bows into a curtain of fog, they eluded their pursuers. They lived to fight another day with less fortunate results.

Whitby, at the mouth of the Yorkshire Esk, has its old, sailor, shipbuilding part and its residential new. Unlike Scarborough, it is content to remain staid and select, rather than progressive as applied to present day, popular, seaside resorts. It is content to wear its old, well-worn livery, rather than adopt the newer styles favoured by tourist and "tripper." Those who have approached it by the coast railway from the North cannot fail to have admired the glorious cliff scenery, with little, hidden fishing-villages nestling in their hollows and dotting the way along. Nor is the route to it by the beautiful valley of the Esk less picturesque, less entrancing. Like Scarborough, like West Hartlepool, it has no fortress-guns, nothing save stout hearts for aggression or defence. The Germans hit out, there was no one, within range, to hit back. There were no soldiers, no wireless station, no entrenched camp, If the men of the town were not killed by bombardment, there was nothing human left for the guns but women and children.

Whitby has its grand, stately Abbey, a landmark on the cliff top, sacred in its ruins. It possesses, too, a museum containing very fine specimens of the huge and terrible forms of life found in the blue lias clay of the neighbourhood. In this clay are the "pockets" of the jet variety of lignite, or coal originating in wood. This fossil substance, once largely used for mourning jewels, is known as Whitby jet.

Half an hour after the two German battleships had bombarded Scarborough, the coastguard at the signal station on the East Cliff saw them coming out of the haze towards the shore. They were steaming at top speed and were half hidden by the spray breaking over their bows. In a few minutes they had come in quite close under the cliffs. This position, so near to the shore, caused their

Mary Street, Hartlepool.

Cleveland Road, Hartlepool.

shells to pass over the cliff. Aimed chiefly at the coast-guard station, they went over and beyond their mark. Whitby was under heavy shell-fire but for a few minutes, but in that time probably some hundred shells were thrown into the town, doing great damage to property, particularly in the Fishburn Park district, behind the railway station. The Abbey, a conspicuous mark, might easily have been demolished, but, though struck by several shells, and its western gateway destroyed, the Germans showed unusual consideration for a relic so sacred. It is interesting to note here that the effect of the bombardment, generally, was to terrorise dogs as to make them wander far from their homes.

As at West Hartlepool and Scarborough, the seafolk of Whitby were not greatly perturbed by their experience of the newer methods of German warfare. They, too, hardly realised what had happened till the firing ceased. Roofs had been torn off, fronts of houses bodily blown in, windows on all sides shattered, three people killed and two wounded, yet there was little or no panic. Most of those who left the town soon returned.

Among those who were killed outright, or died soon afterwards, were:—

> An old goods porter, William Tunmore. He was struck by pieces from an exploding shell while in the cattle dock, and died as he was being conveyed to the hospital.
>
> An invalid lady, Mrs. Miller, was struck by shell splinters while in bed. She afterwards succumbed to her injuries.
>
> An old seaman of 70 years probably died from shock. He was found dead the day following the German attack.

The following is a complete list of those killed during the bombardment:—

WHITBY.

Frederick Randall, R.N.	30
William Edward Tunmore	61
Mrs. Winefride Miller, Spring Hill Terrace	—

IV.

SURMISES AND OPINIONS.

O England! standing with uplifted head
Upon the wind-swept threshold of thy sea, ...
Remember them and theirs, and let thy race,
Under God's hand, strike to their destined goal,
And bring all men God's pity and God's grace.

James Bernard Fagan.

Quite naturally, much conjecture followed upon the raid. After any startling event guess-work is busy. Particularly must this be the case when much that is hidden cannot, for the moment, be made known. The links of Empire are strained in the greatest tug-of-war of all the centuries. A chain of events, plain to some, obscure to others, ridiculed by a great many, had led onward to a world-crisis in which this Empire is playing a chief part—a shaking of the foundations upon which civilisation rests. By it, our national stability must be undermined to its fall or strengthened to its greater glory.

Yarmouth was to have been bombarded in November. Why, we cannot say, except that like most other East coast ports and towns it had nothing, save its own right arm, wherewith to offer any resistance to invasion. The raid upon it failed. The German shell-fire only reached the beach. Yarmouth is naturally protected from the sea by shifting sandbanks. These lie at some distance from the shore. Between them and the mainland are the Yarmouth Roads, like the Downs off Dover, where ships may ride in safety. The Germans, thorough in every military and naval detail, had, of course, charts showing the position of the buoys upon the banks. They knew therefore the exact firing-distance from which they could bombard the town. Either with set purpose or because of the shifting sand, the buoys had been moved further out. The assailing squadron took up position according to chart, but were thereby baulked of their prey. They were out of distance. The aircraft which, in late January, hovered over the port and neighbouring coast, dropping bombs, were of no more military significance, and beyond killing a few more unarmed, peaceful citizens, achieved no commensurate result. York House, the Sandringham country home of our King, might have been the objective of the venture, daring and unscrupulous as it undoubtedly was. But it is within the range of probability that this aircraft-crossing and the bombardment which preceded it was more pretentious. Both might have been directed towards spying out the land, so as to find a way in for some more effective action. This is mere surmise, but we know that the great ones of the earth, who claim an extension of territory for a more picturesque performance of the goose-step, were spreading their gaze for something more tangible than Paris, Calais or Nancy, as a gift for the Emperor's birthday, January 27th. Who knows? Possibly the keepsake was to be a slice of the Durham coalfield, a few of the big and busy manufacturing towns of Yorkshire, or a new shooting-box in the sporting domains of agricultural Norfolk. By ambition fell the angels. When Admiral Beatty, early on the Sabbath morning of January 24th, sank the armoured cruiser, Blucher, let in fire and water upon other battleships, and sent fleeing to their base all that was left of the third raiding squadron, there was enough mischief done to make an archangel fall. And there are such made in Germany. Yet another conjecture. The Good Hope and Monmouth, unflinchingly accepted battle against great odds off the coast of Chili. Ships and crews were sent to the bottom of the Pacific by a German squadron. That was fair fighting. There were no foul blows against women and children, no devastating fire directed upon unprotected towns. That victorious detachment from the German fleet was in turn driven from the Pacific by the Japanese fleet, and, by way of Cape Horn, sought to coal at, or to annex, that extreme outlier of the British Empire, the Falkland Islands, in the South Atlantic. There, Admiral Sturdee unexpectedly intruded upon the scene, with the result that some of the fastest ships and the surest gunners of the enemy's navy were sunk. The loss caused the Emperor much searching of heart. Were the various raids upon the East coast an attempt at a quid pro quo, a tit-for-tat kind of stroke to equalise matters between the two forces after this disaster? Was the descent upon the coast towns a challenge to our North Sea supremacy? If so, Admiral

Tirpitz went once too often to the well. Only by half an
hour and a patch of fog did he escape after his bombardment of the Hartlepools, Scarborough and Whitby. Again,
the object aimed at might have been to cause a panic by
another deed of "frightfulness." What do we read in the
German papers to-day?

> "No means can be too unholy to combat this hideous
> octopus whose tentacles have too long encircled the
> peoples of the world."
> "The British Empire, built up of cards on a crazy
> foundation of deceit, is even now tottering to its fall."
> "The bastard tongue of the canting island pirates must
> be swept back from the place it has usurped, and forced
> into the remotest corners of Britain."

"At every word a reputation dies." Kitchener's new
army is nearly ready. A panic might cause the people
to insist on its being kept at home. A raid would be a
mere curtain-raiser to a full dress performance. Our
million men must stand by the moat to guard the home
citadel. Thus would the "hideous octopus," "the bastard
tongue," cry out.

Once again. It has been urged that the ships which
came in the night and fled in the morning were decoys
to lure on a part of our fleet to destruction by the German
Navy coming out at a safe moment to meet it. And,
it is added, that a part of our pursuing squadron was
actually sandwiched in between the High Sea Fleet and
the returning raiders. If this be true we shall be told
so some day, and also how these units of ours escaped
from that other octopus whose tentacles were so ready to
encircle it.

What splendid emplacements for wide-sweeping 13-inch
or 15-inch guns could be fashioned on the height by
Throston Farm! Their far-reaching aim would search
every square mile of Hartlepool Bay. Indignation has been
aroused because some such guns were not in position when
eight o'clock struck on the eventful morning. But we had
no army ready when we declared war, only a chosen few
of heroic mould to confront the legions that came on like
grasshoppers for multitude. How then could we think
of guns for our inviolate shores! And when we had
entered the zone of fire it was too late to think of fortifying
the shores by such huge weapons. Those that were in

being were needed elsewhere. Moreover, such guns would
need gun-emplacements and bomb-proof shelters. These
are very costly to construct, and would take a long time
to make ready. All the unprotected places on the East
coast would cry out for them. Here would be distraction
from things that more greatly mattered! And where were
the gunners to come from? The biggest of guns require
the most expert handling. Should we take marksmen from
the navy to weaken it? It could not be done. No, the
hardy dwellers by the coast must brave it out. They are
not "canting island pirates." Not the men to squeal if
the enemy trod upon their soil, but unflinching Britons
in the hour of national trial. After all, what was fifty
minutes of shell-fire to the daily hurricane of explosives
that sweeps over the anguished plains of France and
Belgium! The work of the navy has been given out. It
is not to divide itself up for the protection of this or that
section of the coast but, in maintaining our supremacy of
the sea, to annihilate the German Fleet. To give each bit
of the coast its demanded share would be perhaps to give
all to the submarine torpedo. But, possibly, now that the
enemy has made such close acquaintance with us, the duty
to ourselves that far-seeing men tried to impress upon
us, the lessons which more than one war ought to have
enforced, will not go neglected or unheeded.

Before the death-rate was called, before the damage to
property could be counted up, some in their despair were
given to ask where were those particular fighting craft that
were known to be in port. There was a small cruiser of the
Patrol class, a submarine and destroyer. Why didn't they
go out and engage? That is what they really did. The
Patrol shivered under a broadside, the destroyers had
several killed and wounded. But these ships were not
meant to engage battle-cruisers with heavy guns. They
were scouts, whose duty was to find the enemy should he
come, and to tell of his coming. The loss of life goes on
mounting up, the destruction to property was great, but
we, as a people, are to blame. Had the guns been there
the cruisers would not have come, had the army now
being equipped been ready for "The Day," the costliest,
deadliest war of all the ages would never have taken place.

V.

THE BOMBARDMENT.

Heard so oft
In worst extremes, and on the perilous edge
Of battle. *Paradise Lost.*

In the "Merry Wives of Windsor" Shakespere has written "I hope upon familiarity will grow more contempt." Among the other few details we receive from the battlefields of France and Belgium are those which tell us how the pleasant folk of both countries pursue their ordinary work in the fields, gathering in, ploughing up, preparing for late sowing or for the seedtime of spring. Although the streams of human love may be dried up, and everywhere men's hearts quake for fear, yet these trusting labourers believe that harvest will not fail them, that those who sow in tears shall reap in joy. They live in simple faith side by side with the grim scenes of murderous strife, within the sound of the crashing guns, within striking distance of the moaning and whining shells. Like the men who go down to the sea in ships and do their business in great waters, these children of a land full of the rivals who still live, of the tired dead who sleep on unmoved, furrow, drill and smooth out the soil unconcerned.

We, who for long years have lived in towns free from the clash of arms, have not acquired this stolidity, this apparent indifference to the red ruin of war. With a mutinous India, with an armed Transvaal, we have had to fight for continued Imperial existence; but at home, faced on all sides by the battling sea, we have not been disturbed by external foes. We had hope to weld our world-wide Empire together in the bonds of peace and to enjoy its inexhaustible fruits. British democracy was absolutely opposed to conquest or aggressive war. If we continually added to our fleet, it was only because of the threatening rivalry of the German people, who sought to take from us the trident of the seas. Our fleet was our shield. It kept the seas open, not for our exclusive use, but for the peaceful coming and going of the merchantmen of all nations. Other fleets were alike untrammelled. Our army, if perfectly trained and equipped, was insignificant when compared with the conscript forces of Continental Powers. Our wholehearted desire for a peaceful solution of international difficulties led the German militant professors to declare that we had, in our prosperity, lost our old martial spirit, that we were a decadent people ripe for dethronement in position and power. The German Empire, armed to a man, with unscrupulous agents in every zone, with a navy only less in strength than our own, was ready at the word of command to take our office. Our political and domestic dissensions needed, perhaps, some great stroke of fate for us to recover our reason and to consolidate our strength.

Two words, "raid" and "invasion," have been used in connection with the Great War and the side issues to which the bombardments of the East coast belong. The difference in meaning between the two is slight, for a successful raid might, with adequate force, be followed immediately by an invasion. The Danes raided, as well as invaded, our eastern shores. William the Conqueror's invasion in 1066 was followed by the subjugation of the Saxons. A raid may be regarded as an attack by violence; an invasion as hostile entrance into the possessions of another. Raids, and even invasions, have been easier on unfortified coasts by the newer methods of naval warfare adopted in our own day. The Martello Towers, still to be seen on our South coast, could scarcely have offered successul resistance to Napoleon's fleet had it made a descent in force on our shores. And we have seen that, at Liege, Namur, Maubeuge, Antwerp, modern forts, thought to be invulnerable, crumbled and cracked like the shell of a nut under the fierce pressure of the largest types of modern siege artillery, so secretly provided. Nelson effectually blockaded the ports of Northern France where the French army was in waiting to cross the English Channel. In the civil struggle between the northern and southern States of America, to run the blockade with contraband of war meant great gain to the daring. But, with the coming of the submarine, blockades are much more difficult. Battleships, lying-in-wait, are at the mercy of the craft at wait-in-lying. A new experience with them is that, in the darkest night and in the heaviest gale, they can send a "Formidable" and her crew to the bottom with a torpedo blow. Admiral Beatty, in his despatch after the third attempted raid, said he was prevented from following the crippled cruisers of the enemy further because of threatening submarines. We have read of them in our daily papers as operating as far north as the Arctic, as distant from their base as the shores of America. Costly dreadnoughts and cruisers, with expert crews of many years training, cannot be placed at the mercy of these stealthy monsters that can rest in hope on the bed of the sea. And to this peril must be added the even greater one of floating and submerged mines used, as we know to our cost, indiscriminately, by the Germans in our narrow seas. Hundreds of thousands of these buoyant shells must have been for years in the making by the enemy, if the number used and in storage is to be reckoned. This was Germany the peace-loving! It is believed by those best able to judge, that about 1,500 shells were fired by the Seydlitz, Moltke and Blucher, supposing those fighting-ships to have come over, in the attack upon the Hartlepools. But a considerable number of these were fired into the sea. The attacking flotilla was fearful of the terror that lurketh in darkness—the slim submarine—and sought to keep it at bay. The only possible defence of the East coast under the new conditions was by heavy guns in hidden emplacements. The Hague Convention, which to the German Junker was only another "scrap of paper," had decided that "unfortified towns shall not be subjected to bombardment with naval armament." So, with the fleet in suspended animation, except for the patrol, fast battle-cruisers could, at 25 to 28 knots an hour, come in the night and practically bombard with impunity. They first came on the afternoon of November 2nd. Yarmouth was their objective. Their mission was to lay waste the town, to provoke some section of the British Fleet to pursue them, to sow mines broadcast had their ships to flee for shelter. If no angry squadron followed, then the mines would be in the way of neutral ships and of trawlers, and ensure the destruction of any craft that might unsuspectingly strike them. These were the intentions, these the tactics followed in the raid and intercepted raid that came after.

Back Rugby Terrace, West Hartlepool.

Railway Damage at West Hartlepool.
(See page 97)

Failure marked the first raid, failure and partial destruction of the invading ships, the last. Sandbanks and mines saved the herring town. Many men, experienced in naval and military matters, had believed that any such minatory incursion would be doomed to failure. Wireless telegraphy would, they said, at once bring help to the attacked and cut off from their base the ruthless wreckers. This confidence was misplaced. Not only did a detached squadron demonstrate its ability to cross the North Sea from Heligoland to Yarmouth, worming its way through mine-fields and evading our fleet, but it proved that, under more favourable conditions, it had the power to work mischief. It emboldened Admiral Tirpitz to try again.

Beyond its success as a demonstration, the Yarmouth venture resulted in neither loss of life or destruction of property to the threatened town. Submarine, D 5, struck a mine when in pursuit of the enemy and was lost. The German ship, Yorck, struck a mine on the journey back and went down with a loss of 300 lives. If the Seydlitz, Moltke and Von der Tann were there with their 11-inch guns, they were never nearer than ten miles from the shore. 18,000 yards, or about ten miles, is the range of an 11-inch gun. It is interesting to note here that many people in the Hartlepools during the morning of the bombardment said they could hear, and see, the largest shells as they passed over their heads. The whirr and slam were, of course, sufficiently pronounced, but to see the shell in its flight would be impossible. If you stand immediately behind a gun, as the shell is discharged from it, you may see a dark spot following in the line of its flight. This is the cleavage, the displacement, the passage made in the air as the shell wings its way towards the target, whatever that might be. Sir Admiral Percy Scott, in a description of modern gunfire, said that the projectile from a 12-inch gun would take but twelve seconds to reach its destination five miles away. Would the eye be able to follow it at any part of its course, travelling at that velocity? Sir Percy adds that a 12-inch shot, fired at a range of fifteen miles, would reach an altitude of 22,500 feet, or 7,500 feet above the summit of Mont Blanc. In the bombardment of the Hartlepools the German ships

fired 11-inch, 8-inch, and 20-pounder shells. "The 12-inch
gun, such as the New Zealand and Indomitable mount,
weighs about sixty tons, will penetrate eight inches of
armour at thirteen miles, strikes a blow sufficient to raise
by as much as one foot no less than 53,000 tons—equivalent
to the weight of two battle-cruisers—discharges a shot six
times the weight of what hosiers call 'a small man,' and
costs at least £100 each time it is fired." This is given here
because it illustrates better than anything else can, except
the wrecked streets and the poor, maimed limbs, the terrible
nature of the murderous fire that for forty minutes was
rained upon the batteries and two towns in the dawn of
December 16, 1914. To the brave Commander and to the
men in the batteries and trenches we take off our hats.
Little has been said in commendation of their conduct,
yet they bore the full blast of a terrifying ordeal, never
once flinched, and hit back with effect.

Looking east from the high ground on which Tunstall
Manor, a residence of Mr. William Cresswell Gray (now
Sir William Cresswell Gray, Bart.), is built, one is
able on a clear day to take in a broad sweep of
the town below, of the bay beyond, and of the ancient
borough on its flank. This was an admirable point of
vantage on that grey morning, when a mist hung over the
water, to see the Hartlepools for the first time in their
history under shell fire. As the great cruisers at the command
of the almighty Emperor came in from the east, only
silhouettes of their dark forms could be seen. They had
a murderous message to deliver. "He who is with God
is always in the majority," said His Majesty later. One
would think the fiend that was "hurled, flaming from the
ethereal skies," was more frequently at his side. The guns
opened fire. Long flashes burst through the haze, the roar
was deafening as the batteries replied. Then the gasworks
flamed up and shells hurtled overhead. It was a dangerous
spot, well within the zone of storms. Yet, there stood
one with some of his family and a staff of workers,
brought in haste together by the fury of the blast that
had broken upon the inhabitants of the towns at their feet.
It was very dangerous ground, but at first they dimly
understood the meaning of it all, and scarcely realised

the perilous nature of the position on which they stood. Unexploded shells found in the fields just beyond were afterwards fired by the military. The nose of one 11-inch monster, many pounds in weight, was found near conservatories not a hundred yards away. Still, on that morning they saw the whole tragic drama through, fascinated by the moving figures that hurled out their hatred.

This attitude of mind was, I think, characteristic of the great majority. The workings of the minds of very few at that moment led them to conclude that blows were to descend upon them like thunderbolts. True, there was nothing in history like the world-combat going on, day by day, outside. The issues at stake, the number of troops engaged, the destructive forces let loose made it a tragedy that surpassed all others. The vanity of the Kaiser was, perhaps, appeased by the thought. We, as a people, were outside the limit of Continental brawls and battles. Between our neighbours and ourselves there was a great gulf fixed.

When the cannon gave their shout of hatred, at first with distant feebleness, anon with a nearer roar, when the batteries answered back in notes of defiance, then people awoke and said, "There is a naval engagement off the coast." At the ancient borough, minds were rapidly made up as to the true meaning of the crackling salvoes. Around the Town Moor, and in a line with it landwards, the outburst of furious hatred staggered every household, while to right and left shivered glass and shaking tenements told that the foe had come. It had been said many times by those best able to judge, that such nerve-racking happenings were to be expected but, strange to add, none were told what to do were the worst to overtake them. If there was panic, followed by a more dangerous flight, no one could wonder. Some at West Hartlepool, on hearing the guns, made for Newburn Bridge, fully persuaded that a naval engagement, near at hand, was in progress. The answering batteries confirmed this, more or less, general opinion. One who was there told how he saw the local "Patrol," small cruiser and submarine outside the breakwater, bravely engaging the enemy, pigmies against giants. Big shells were throwing up huge splashes all around them. Broadsides hurled their missiles

at them, and presently they had to retire, bruised but
not broken. When a huge shell ploughed up the sidings
beyond the bridge and other shells began to find the
whereabouts of goods station and main line railway then,
quite undeceived as to the true character of the firing,
those on the bridge retired to safer quarters. It would
be easy to give many instances of miraculous escapes.
A man and his wife were looking out of their bedroom
window when a chimney opposite collapsed under the
impact of a twenty-pounder. A huge gap was made in the
roof, from which smoke and dust escaped. The bedclothes
and pillows were pierced by jagged fragments of metal.
The household had only just before gone below.

Germany had perfected her organisation in its every
detail. Her intelligence Department had eyes and ears
for every plan, for every secret. Her spies were in every
nook and corner of the occupied world. The three battle-
cruisers, told off to give one bit of glamour to the sleeping
eyes of her languid fleet, knew exactly where best to take
up position against the opposing fort so as to save their
skins. The Blucher, now at peace from the surging tide
of conflict, was there to take its appointed place. In the
German report of the raid it was stated that " We received
some slight damage." That, in " Censor " language, meant
a great deal. Since the abortive third raid, we learn that
the stricken ship had eleven casualties. Those best capable
of seeing the effects of the batteries' fire say that lyddite.
shell, more than once, swept the enemy's decks. Quite
possibly the Von der Tann, absent from the third essay,
needed overhauling on her return home. The bomb-dropping
from aircraft on the Norfolk coast was, probably, a mere
" blind." The Intelligence Department of Admiral Tirpitz
was not quite sure that the Lion and Tiger were fast
asleep in some sheltered lair. The aircraft were sent to
see. They reported that the coast was clear. Then the
Lion and Tiger came into their own.

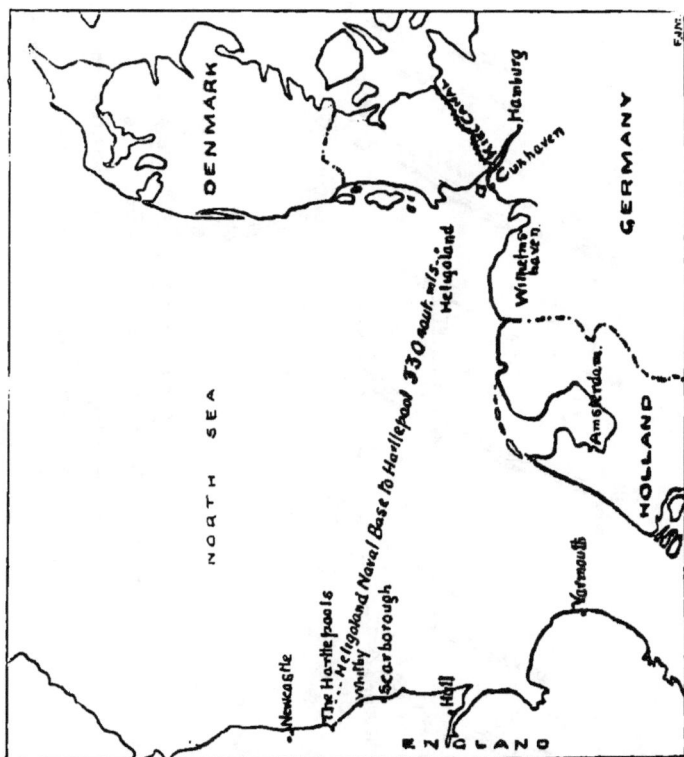

About 370 statute miles north-west of Heligoland, or twelve hours by the fastest cruisers, lies the Port of Hartlepool, almost on the river boundary between Durham and Yorkshire. At 8-10 a.m.. on the Wednesday of December 16, 1914, after an unmolested night-run across the North Sea, three German warships sailed into Hartlepool Bay and confronted the batteries on the shore.

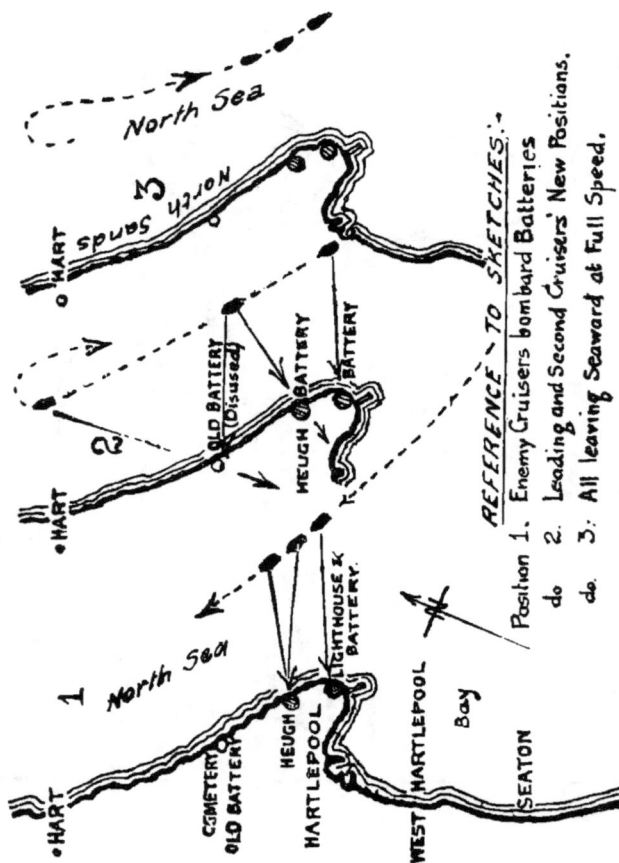

REFERENCE TO SKETCHES:-

Position 1. Enemy Cruisers bombard Batteries.

do   2. Leading and Second Cruisers' New Positions.

do   3. All leaving Seaward at Full Speed.

F.J.T.

Varying positions of attacking Cruisers.

They had carefully chosen the night for their journey, the hour of their arrival. The mists of the morning had not yet been dispelled by the sun, which later shone out with rare December brilliancy. Before the ships broke through the curtain of haze which concealed them, heavy firing was heard out at sea. Flashes of flame could be seen, but nothing else. The coastguards thought our own fleet was engaged. As they came nearer, their dark outlines loomed up distinctly, but it was not possible to read their names. They were flying the "Eagle" ensign which, in the dimness of the dawn, could not be easily distinguished from our own White Ensign. The fainter salvoes had been enough to awaken the heavy sleepers. The louder, ear-splitting roar, punctuated by the deep boom of the 11-inch gun, brought wondering people down stairs to find those who were already up in the streets or on the Town Moor. There was no doubt now in the minds of the watchers as to the meaning of it all. The Germans had come with the fastest and fittest of their new fleet. The Hartlepools was a defended port, though the West Hartlepool part of it was absolutely without a gun. But Germans at war do not make nice distinctions. They deem themselves privileged to hack or pound their way through soldiers and citizens, the pugnacious and the peaceful.

If our own guns north and south of the bay were too limited in their range to be effective at great distances, or against 11-inch Krupp cemented armour, yet precautions had been taken against attack or invasion. The local mind had not satisfied itself that either was probable. Those in authority had long thought that a raid at least was to be expected when time favoured. Responsible officers were always on the alert at the Lighthouse and Heugh forts.

Word was passed to the harbour for the patrol flotilla to be ready. It seems almost grotesque that the destroyer Doon, the small cruiser Hardy and a submarine should venture to engage such monster craft as the Moltke, Seydlitz, Derfflinger, Blucher, Von der Tann, any three of which might certainly oppose them. But they did. The result was not long in doubt. Broadsides were opened on them. The Doon, with two killed and seven wounded, the Hardy, with three killed and fifteen wounded should, with better gunnery, have been sunk. As it was, their only prospect of keeping afloat was in escape. And escape they did.

At about 4,000 yards or 2¼ miles, the leading ship of the three opened fire. Of the three shots thus directed at the battery, one struck it, a second went to the right, killing several men, and the third, aimed too high, wrecked the upper floor of the house occupied by the Misses Kay, both of whom were killed. The rear ship was 2,000 yards further out to sea. As the squadron swung curving in all three concentrated their fire on the fort which, with rare courage, replied. In a German sailor's letter, which appeared in the *Northern Daily Mail* a month after the raid, we read that his ship did not get back to Kiel until December 17, the day following the bombardment. This delay was probably due to the funnels having been shot away by the lyddite shells of the battery, thereby reducing speed. Quite possibly this ship was the battle-cruiser, Von der Tann.

From private information since received, it would appear that the Blucher, sunk in the third attempted raid, did actually take part in the bombardment of the Hartlepools. She was left to continue the attack on the batteries when the two leading ships moved by way of the North Sands towards the old Cemetery Battery.

According to the accounts of some of her survivors, she was somewhat badly damaged by the guns of the batteries and had a couple of 6-inch or 5.9 inch guns knocked endways. Ten men of her crew were killed and several wounded. She returned to Kiel to refit, and only came out again in time to be sunk.

The troops on duty on this terribly trying morning were two companies of the Durham Royal Garrison Artillery, under Lieut.-Col. Robson, an old Volunteer officer, an ex-Mayor of West Hartlepool, and still an Alderman of the Corporation of that town. He was fire commander when the shell-storm burst. Col. Robson was subsequently decorated by King George on the occasion of the visit of the King and Queen Mary to the shipyards and works of the port, June 15, 1917. The actual investiture with the insignia of a Companion of the most distinguished Order of St. Michael and St. George took place in the Old Yard of Sir William Gray, Bart., and was, as officially

The Officers and Men of the R.G.A. and Durham R.G.A. who manned the Batteries at Hartlepool.
(See page 70)

Other Members of the Durham R.G.A. who manned the guns.
(See page 70)

Railway Chair—Relic of Bombardment found in Chimney of
28, Mainsforth Terrace, West Hartlepool.
(See page 129)

announced, "for distinguished services rendered during
the war." Beyond this he has twice been mentioned
in despatches. It was a fiery ordeal by which the
courage of the gun squad was tested. Made up of young
Territorials never before in action, they stood to their
guns like veterans. With 6-inch against 11-inch and 8-inch
guns they were hopelessly handicapped. The batteries
were continually hit in front and flank, but not a man was
displaced. With such a concentrated fire upon them it
would seem almost impossible for this to have been so.
Skilfully manœuvring their ships to elude the torpedoes
of any submarine craft that might attack them, the Germans
engaged at too close range for a dropping fire to be
effective. The haze had made their nearness necessary,
and thus their shots went straight to the battery mark.
Under different atmospheric conditions, and with perhaps
greater accuracy of aim, the battery would, in all
probability, have been wiped out. As it was, the shells
went over and beyond the Town Moor, causing great
destruction to property and loss of life. The Territorial
gunners, with a few old hands to stiffen them in their
deadly work, held grimly on to their task and gave a
parting salvo to the intruding Huns as they turned away
to the east.

With a shivering of glass and a grazed mark on its
masonry, the Lighthouse, erected in 1847, sustained no
greater damage. The ships, inward or outward bound, can
still wave to it "their silent welcomes and farewells."
Though shells hurtled through the air to the right and left
of it, though the ground buildings around it were demolished,
it remained standing erect as the most prominent structure
along the sea front. We may be sure the Germans had
accurate maps of the two towns before them as they
blazed away. Every building in their eyes meet for
destruction had, we may be equally certain, been carefully
marked. If, as prisoners from the Blucher have stated,
they lost their bearings through fog and made the Yorkshire
and Durham, instead of the Northumbrian coast, the same
conclusion applies. The German staff know the highways
and byeways of this country as well as they do those of
France and Belgium. In the conquest of the world, you
must know your way. Delays are dangerous. Possibly

the Lighthouse was spared because it was a good guide-line for gun-laying. So many degrees to the right of it, so many to the left, and, approximately, the mark sought for would be found.

West Hartlepool's turn was to come next. Pilots on board, or spies on the shore, lent a helping hand to guide two out of the three ships towards a favoured position from which they could the more accurately distribute their favours over the younger town. The rear ship was left to pour broadsides at the battery, while the leading ships swung round towards the old Hartlepool Cemetery to take up a new position from which to direct, with the remaining ship, what seems to have been four separate lines of fire. For forty minutes the two towns were under continuous bombardment. Then the two ships rejoined their companion and together they steamed swiftly away. Those best able to judge, estimate that, in the sea and over the land, not less than 1,500 shells were fired. If, on an average, each shell cost £50 in the making, £75,000 must, approximately, have been thrown into air and water in forty minutes, or at the rate of £1,875 every minute. O, the waste of insensate war! O, the madness of insatiable ambition! Some such huge sum was squandered in the destruction of man's industrious labour, in the maiming, distorting and effacing of a God-given image.

In addition to the men of the D.R.G.A., infantrymen were on duty occupying positions around the batteries. These were under the command of Major Tristram and consisted of half the County Battalion. Subjected to a tempest of shells, these British braves stood their ground at every point.

One company of the 3rd Yorkshires, under Captain Rolls, occupied the trenches at Seaton Carew. A detachment of the Durham Fortress Royal Engineers (Jarrow), under Captain Williams, was on duty at various points of the defences.

The armament of the ships engaged certainly exceeded 100 guns, of which probably 75 per cent. were in action. Firing broadsides of high-explosive shell from port or starboard with 11-inch, 8-inch, and 6-inch guns, loss of life among the defending force was inevitable. Of the County Battalion, four men were killed and ten wounded in the trenches. A number of engineers were also wounded by shell fire. With the bombardment over, the troops, undaunted by an experience trying even to seasoned troops, gallantly led the way to the wrecked homes around, there to rescue the wounded and remove the dead.

Fishing and pilot boats in the bay, between the ships and the batteries, were not struck, the shells passing over them. It should be placed on record how two infantry sergeants went to the rescue of a fisherman who had broken his leg in hurriedly getting out of his boat. This they did under heavy fire.

VI.

RESULTS OF THE BOMBARDMENT.

Ruin seize thee, ruthless King!
Confusion on thy banners wait!
Though fann'd by Conquest's crimson wing,
They mock the air with idle state.
The Bard.

Germany has taught the nations how to fight a new kind
of rearguard action at sea, as she scuttles away in seven
league boots behind the great rock, Heligoland, we were
foolish enough to make over to her. She sows explosive
mines broadcast from her gallant craft as, nervy, she
makes haste home. Her War-lords and professor-scientists
have revolutionized modern methods of war, but these have
left them only as brainy barbarians. The people of the
Hartlepools listened with a strained attention as the guns
roared out their coming. As the shells tore their way with
a rending scream they knew them as messengers of death.
As the deafening crack of explosion followed, it was little
wonder if some hesitated, some ran, others stood still.
The storm burst, the thunder boomed; thereafter followed
a great calm. The last broadside was answered by a
parting salvo from the undaunted few, and the chosen
might of naval Germany filed away to the north-east,
mine-sowers endangering pursuit. The sudden break-off in
the fierce tumult was as startling as its coming. We shall
know the whole truth some day, but we can imagine the
wireless operators on board receiving a message—"Run
for your lives! Beatty is hard on your trail!" We know
now that the Admiral had his chimneys on fire, as he tried
his best's best to come alongside. A stray cloud got in
his line of sight and shut out the runaways from view.
On a clear Sabbath morn, a month afterwards, he was right
on the mark.

76

The minefield was responsible for the loss off Flamborough Head, of the collier Ellwater, of the Norwegian Vaaren, off Whitby, and of the Princess Olga, off Scarborough. It was a long and perilous task for the minesweepers to rid a wide area of the sea of these night and noonday terrors.

With the wind from the north-east, the sound of the firing was carried as far as Richmond in Yorkshire. Two miles from Stockton a certain man was in bed when the firing began. All his doors shook violently. His wife called to him upstairs to know what he was about. " I am doing nothing,' 'he said, " Well," she answered, " all the doors of the house are rattling violently." " Put a plug in 'em," he called out, and went on with his sleep. Whether the pheasants at Wynyard were alert and alarmed at the noise, as they were said to have been in Lincolnshire during the January naval fight, we have not been told, but the roof-loving sparrows of the Hartlepools all forsook their homes and fled.

Shell-fire is so mutilating and fatal because of the great number of flying fragments hurtled through the air with killing force as the projectile explodes. Phosphorus is used in the composition of these shells to render them more brittle, more fragmentary as they burst. It poisons the wound made by the jagged splinter, invariably delays healing, and often leads to fatal results. So the toll of dead increased.

A little girl brought her school prize-book for her teacher to see. It had come under shell-fire as it stood in its place at home. A fragment had pierced the cover and gone through 182 pages of the child's book. There it was brought up, and remained fixed to the last page it had pierced. A rail on the line between West Hartlepool and Seaton Carew was cut in two, as clean as if a knife had severed it. A bricklayer was called in to rebuild a chimney that a 20-pounder had brought down. He completed his work. The fire was lit, but the smoke would not ascend. The workman thought a brick had got wedged in it. He opened the chimney and, below the repairs, he found a railway chair that had been heaved high in the air to fall down the chimney, blocking the way. Enterprising tradesmen in Church Street, West Hartlepool, exhibited in their windows shell-noses and shell-bases of great thickness and weight. These helped onlookers to form some idea of the "Jack Johnsons" and "Black Marias" with which our unwavering troops have been pelted in the French and Belgian trenches. Many fragments have been allowed to remain in doors and window frames as reminders of a troubled morning, and many unexploded shells found a safe resting-place in distant fields, where they were afterwards exploded by the military, or brought back to barracks. The smallest fragments were in certain stages of their flight violently effective. The new reinforced-concrete wall on the Clarence Road was pierced through by bits not much larger than duck-shot, leaving the expanded metal framework still standing in position.

It was providential that the passenger railway stations of the two towns, crowded, as they were by terror-stricken people—parents and children—should have been free from the fiercest of the fire which shattered houses and streets. The 8-27 a.m. train, from West Hartlepool to Leeds, escaped almost certain destruction by a finger's end. The last carriage was barely clear of the station when a shot came tearing through its northern boundary wall, making a huge hole and covering the down platform beneath it with broken bricks. Portions of the exploded bomb were thrown forwards across the line with such force as to smash the panels and glass of a carriage attached to a train standing in the dock.

A boy came as usual for the breakfast of a foreman at the shipyards. He was despatched with it just after the enemy opened fire. The poor lad had almost reached his destination, when fragments of a shell, apparently aimed at the gasworks, struck him down and killed him. Near by stands the Scandinavian Church. Its front, facing the tramline, received a sidelong blast of metal hail, which scarred its masonry and left it windowless. A circular piece of thick steel on the deck of a ship, lying in dock, received a clean cut which almost divided it in two, the shell-fragment passing on with sufficient force to kill one of the crew.

Just as the health of many people had been permanently injured by shock, or so nerve-strained as to cause death, so the concussion threw doors, firegrates and house fittings out of plumb in numbers of instances. Bottles of liquor, placed in a row on the shelf of a public-house near the docks, played a bumping tune for half an hour against the plate glass in front of them. The glass remained unbroken, but the front of the house three weeks afterwards began to bulge forwards, and had to be timbered-up.

Though much indiscriminate firing accompanied the movements of the battleships, there seems to have been some method in the madness of the German gunners. Now and then they ran amok, so to speak, and hit out right and left against all and sundry. The Germans proved themselves impartial barbarians. When reason was in evidence, it showed its controlling force in the selection of certain definite lines of fire; when the barbarian was uppermost, then everyone among 100,000 people was a much-hated Britisher, whose speedy withdrawal from active service was best hastened by mutilation or death. A war of extermination is strictly in accordance with German ideas of development. We can almost hear the Emperor, in one of his many homilies to his infatuated people, saying: "Be fruitful and multiply and replenish the earth, but only with Vaterland stock."

Great was the desire of motorists and pedestrians from outside the borough to see with their own eyes the effects of shell-fire upon the port. Shell relic-hunters came, too, all anxious to become the proud possessors of the largest or most jagged fragments. The price of shell went up. The supply was not equal to the demand. Human nature is so curious and so difficult to satisfy in things destructive and ghastly that the purveyors of these outward and visible signs of the methods of barbarism will probably live in hopeful anticipation of another visit from the raiders.

This prevailing state of mind among some was amusingly illustrated in a case heard at the County Court. It was one of disputed ownership. A bouncing piece of shell found rest, but not safety, on private property. Somebody saw it, as it fell heated with all the fire of German hatred.

Regarded with a sort of national pride, it was picked up
and carried off as a Teutonic treasure. A legal estimate
of its present market value varied between £25, £35 and
£40. It is hard even now to decide who was the rightful
owner of this bolt from the blue. The judge, himself,
seemed to recognise the difficulty, though in the end he
decided against the shell-snatcher. To His Honour it
appeared that the Emperor of all the Germans was the
rightful owner.

If, in his wisdom, he had thought right to decide otherwise than he did, no one would have been surprised. Had
he said "This specimen must remain in court until we
have written to the Emperor. He will be told that certain
property of his has been found on the estate of a gentleman
in West Hartlepool. And, it will be added, that if he does
not appear in person to claim it within fourteen days the
property will be sold to pay expenses." In this way the
disputants might have had the great joy of taking the
Sea Lord round to view the results of his handiwork, and the
Corporation the honour of afterwards entertaining him to
a banquet.

Three months after the bombardment an auction sale,
unique in the annals of the town, was held at West
Hartlepool. Nothing of like character made in Germany
and distributed in England was ever before put up for
the competition of bidders. Krupps would probably strike
and further imperil the safety of the German Empire were
they to know that their best phosphoretted mixture had
been subjected to such mercenary antagonism. From the
extensive collections of a local tradesman grim relics of
the December attack upon the port were offered for sale.
For the complete nose of an 11-inch projectile, £6 was
offered and declined. This fragment weighed 97 lb. A more
subdued nose, weighing 24 lb., fetched £4/12/6. Smaller
specimens brought varying prices from 5/- upwards, but
several were withdrawn. These bombardment souvenirs
had been exhibited for some time and had attracted large
crowds.

When the two leading ships left their companion ship
to continue the attack on the batteries, they took up new
positions. One of them went in a north-westerly direction

Hartlepool Union Workhouse.

(See page 83)

Interior of Baptist Chapel, Hartlepool.

by the North Sands, until nearly opposite to Hart Railway Station. The other faced what was once the Cemetery Battery, and both, thereupon, recommenced firing. It may have been that their maps, upon which were marked the site of the old battery, led them to believe that, as at the Heugh and Lighthouse, a garrison force was in occupation. Receiving no response to their attack, where none was possible, they selected other marks inland on which to direct their shell fire.

Following a map of the town and district, one can now apparently trace four distinct lines of fire. Allowance must be made to the right and left of these lines for the movements of the ships, as they turned round to fire from port or starboard, or as they manœuvred rapidly to prevent the successful attack of a possible submarine. They quite likely knew of the barracks at Tunstall Court, Lord Furness's one-time West Hartlepool residence, and tried to reach them. Shots, we know, were continually passing over the high ground above the Park and dropping in the open country beyond. Several unexploded shells were afterwards found on Mr. Robson's farm. One dropped over the stables at "Ambleside" and killed Mr. W. Ropner's cook.

The second line was by way of the Workhouse. Mr. G. E. Usher, the Master of the Workhouse, in his subsequent report to the Guardians of the Hartlepool Poor Law Union, included the following statement:—

On December 16th, at about 8 a.m., the Workhouse came under the shell-fire of a squadron of the German Fleet. It is probable that one of the first German shells sent on its way to land in England burst on the roof of the School's dining-hall. It did considerable damage both to the Schools and the Infirm Block. Only five minutes previous to the explosion about ninety old people were congregated in the dining-hall for religious service.

It is not possible, at least now, to tell the exact number of shells that fell on the Workhouse or in its immediate vicinity. The lowest estimate is twelve, the highest fifty. Huge, weighty fragments from these

missiles, said by experts to have come from the
"Blucher," have been picked up and kept as reminders
of their murderously destructive power.

Damage was done to the north wall of the old
hospital and to the roof of the boys' ward in the
infirmary.   No inmate here happily sustained any
injury.

Naturally, there was panic, especially amongst the
Female Mental cases, but this was of short duration.
The inmates, generally, acted with bravery and
fortitude, while the officers of the institution did their
duty like seasoned soldiers, regardless of personal
danger.

As soon as the bombardment ceased, all the patients
from numbers 2 and 3 Wards were removed to the
Convalescent Block.   The institution was now prepared
to receive a hundred wounded.   In all, fifty-two
wounded patients were brought in, five of whom died.
The doctors and nurses worked as only men and women
work when the lives of their fellows depend upon their
self-sacrifice and skill.   Operations to the number of
thirteen were performed by Dr. Ainsley, assisted by
Drs. English and Macgill.

The death roll ultimately included five inmates :—

Wheelwright, Bewick, age 15 years, died Dec. 30, 1914.
Skelton, Amos   ,, 53   Dec. 26, 1914..
Mossom, Thomas   ,, 54   Jan. 15, 1915.
Ambrose, Robert   ,, 34   Jan. 22, 1915.
Wood, Martha   ,, 6   Feb. 7, 1915..

Distinguished visitors to the wrecked scene
included : The Dean of Durham and Mrs. Hensley
Henson, the Bishop of Jarrow, Lady Londonderry,
Generals Plummer and Kenny, Colonel Tuckey, the
Mayor and Mayoress (Councillor J. R. and Mrs. Fryer)
of West Hartlepool, Mr. Howard Gritten and Sir
Walter and Lady Runciman.

In this second line of fire can be included:—

Jesmond Road Schools.
North Cemetery.
Richardson Street.
Collingwood Road.
Sandringham Road.
Blake Street.
Stephen Street.
Granville Avenue.
Christopher Street.
Bright Street.
Sheriff Street.

Mulgrave Road.
Alma Street.
Grosvenor Street.
Murray Street.
Milton Street.
Grange Road.
Hutton Avenue.
Park Road.
Grasmere Street.
Thirlmere Street.
Keswick Street.

Ashgrove Avenue, to Stranton Grange, where the new Cemetery wall was damaged, and to Brierton Lane.

The third line of fire seems to have been directed towards:—

The Cement Works.
Gas Works, No 2.
Corporation Tram Depôt, Cleveland Road.
May Street.
Brougham Terrace.
Raby Road.
Moore Street.
Gas and Water Works.
Scandinavian Church.
Lower end of Milton Street.
"Northern Daily Mail" Offices.
Wesley Church.
Johnson Street.
Avenue Road, to
Lister Street.

Crimdon Street.
Dene Street.
Lynnfield Schools.
The Tips.
Belk Street.
Mill House Inn.
Rugby Terrace.
Lowthian Road.
Hunter Street.

The fourth line appears to have included:—

Richardson and Westgarth's Engineering Works.
Irvine's (Middleton) Shipyard.
The Docks.
Dock Street.
The West Hartlepool Railway Station.

Church Street.
Dover Street.
Ward-Jackson Hotel.
Whitby and Scarborough Streets.
Lamb Street.
The Goods Station.
Mainsforth Terrace, and the main line, with timber
    sidings, to Seaton Carew.

This may appear fanciful to some, but allowances being
made for erratic firing, along these four lines is to be
located most of the property that sustained serious damage.
As at Hartlepool, the main business thoroughfares escaped
with little injury.

Gas, as well as water, is almost one of the necessaries of
life to the inhabitants of our towns, large and small. For
though to a considerable extent supplemented by electricity,
it will continue to give light, heat and power to the great
majority of our people for many generations. The large
gasholders and water-tower are prominent objects from
almost any local standpoint. Their huge forms would
loom up out of the haze on that memorable morning, when
the Hartlepools awoke to the fact that war had descended
upon them. In the breaking of the world's peace by a
continental power, the east and south coasts of Britain,
from their geographical position, will always be face to
face with the aggressor, should he hazard the great venture
of bringing forces to attack them. Perhaps, after all, it
was as well that the German guns should shower their
explosives upon us. It proved their desperation, it clinched
our determination. In forty minutes our insularity was a
dream of the past. Science had bridged the North Sea with
a startling rapidity.

Of the greater institutions and concerns put out of their
normal stride by the bombardment were the Carnegie
Library, the Goods Station in Mainsforth Terrace, Richardson, Westgarth and Co's. Engineering Works, the Shipyards,
and the Gas and Water Works. A feeling of insecurity
was naturally present in all factories and workshops where
men and women were employed, and in most of them work
was broken or suspended for the rest of the day. Of these,

by far the most important to the community of the port, as a whole, were the gas and water works in Cleveland Road. German kultur, lit up by the torch of a brutal militarism, will be consumed in the conflagration of its own making. One of the lesser lights by which its progress and our own national mind were illumined was the flame from the stricken gasholders. It is strange that the German report of their runaway achievement should dwell with a consuming joy on having put the Parliamentary Borough in momentary darkness. For, considering that all these holders were struck, and the gas in two of them set on fire, there was only a momentary stoppage of the supply. The company controlling it rose to the occasion with praiseworthy promptitude and resource. The two towns were without gaslight on the Wednesday and Thursday following the attack, but on Friday a partial supply was forthcoming, and though handicapped by the complete destruction of the water-gasholder and the partial destruction of another holder, the Company has continued to maintain a sufficient pressure for ordinary purposes. Gasholder No. 2, to which reference has been made, was perforated on the sides by some 250 shell-fragments, the crown by 60 more. Plates were buckled, huge holes, from which the flames leaped, were made. The water-tower was struck, but not seriously, and was immediately made secure.

Seeing that a very considerable staff is employed in the offices and yards of these works, it is more than gratifying to know that so few were fatally or partially injured by the concentrated fire. Mr. Askew, a workman, was killed, another workman seriously injured in Middleton Road. When the engine-room and the boiler-house at the water works were struck, both engine-man and fireman were badly wounded. Mr. Abbott, one of the Company's book-keepers, who lives in Brougham Terrace, received injuries from a shell which burst inside his house. The number of marks and perforations visible upon the plates of the gasholders is a striking illustration of the wide area covered by exploded shell. The Company's claim of indemnity was for £7,500.

Shells, like rifle-bullets, fired at comparatively short distances from the target, whatever that may be, have little or no trajectory, that is they pursue a straight course to the object aimed at. At long range, the shell or bullet in its flight describes a greater or less curve, according to the angle at which the weapon is tilted. This angle in the rifle is regulated by the " sight." The curve may be illustrated by the ribs of an umbrella, the shot following one rib to its greatest height, represented by the ferrule-point at the pointed end of the stick handle, and then, dropping by the rib beyond until it reaches its mark.

At the opening of the session of the Keighley Association of Engineers, October, 1917, Mr. James Meredith, of Armstrong, Whitworth & Co., described the make-up of a latest pattern 12-in. or 15-in. gun. Passing on to powders, he mentioned that the use of a slow burning explosive had entailed the lengthening of the gun. Four times as powerful as gunpowder, cordite developed a temperature of 8,000 degrees Fahrenheit. The pressure behind the shell, about 40,000lb. to the square inch (developing by the explosion a heat at which diamonds melted and carbon boiled), sent the projectile at a speed of 25 miles per minute, reaching its target before the sound of its firing. The high explosive with which the missile achieved its work came almost entirely from coal-tar products, and a slight alteration of the shell-nose would add a mile to the carrying power. Mr. Meredith had something to say on the enemy's use of dirigibles and aeroplanes in their raids on this country, and gave reasons for the belief that this means of attack was being overcome. Returning to the guns, Mr. Meredith said the range of the 12-inch gun was about 17 miles, and ten miles at sea was recognised as the fighting range. A 15-inch gun would cover 27 miles, the distance being traversed in $1\frac{3}{4}$ minutes, and even 34 miles could be reached. The German gun, which gave trouble at Dunkirk with a range of 25 miles, would go down, built on their system, to a range of about $12\frac{1}{2}$ miles after firing 50 rounds. This was not the case with our guns—for reasons which it would not be prudent to give. In fact, our guns, both field and naval, were now second to none in this war.

It has been pointed out that the three battle-cruisers, on taking up position about two miles a little to the north of the Hartlepool batteries, directed their fire upon them. When their guns were tilted ever so little the shots went over. The result we know. Where the curve was great, their flight was as far as Greenside, beyond Trimdon, and within two miles of Sedgefield. When the angle was reduced, shells fell at Embleton and Pudding Poke. With a still further reduction, they dropped in the fields beyond Elwick, near the inn beyond the Three Gates, at Dalton Piercy, at North Urn, near Brierton Moor House and, nearer home still, at Stranton Grange, where the New Cemetery wall was damaged. The extreme limit reached would therefore be about ten miles. The shells, falling in the soft fields, did not explode, and caused but little trouble. Several of them were afterwards on view in front of the barracks at Staincliffe. The West Hartlepool Corporation would like to place them in the Public Library as reminders to future generations of the Great War in which so many sons of the town and district took part, and of the raid in which so many lives were sacrificed.

The shells which just overtopped the batteries had the adjacent homes, and the lives of those in them, at their mercy. The tenderest mercies of an exploding shell are cruel beyond conception. It was the shell-fire of overpowering artillery, rather than the furious onset of the foe, that compelled French's army to retreat at Mons upon Paris. It was 11-in., 8-in. and 6-in. shells that tore off and broke through the roofs and walls of some of the stoutest buildings of Hartlepool. Their scattered fragments killed, shattered, maimed, wherever human beings came between them and their flight. When the stretchers brought in the victims, self-sacrificing doctors, face to face as they are every day with death, were unnerved and pallid at the mangled, limbless forms laid out on the operating tables before them.

Misguided, or intentional firing, led to huge gaps being made in the Promenade and in the bank behind it. Some of these holes were of immense size, grim reminders of even bigger ones across the Channel. Seats and chairs were smashed, the café ruined, the Rugby football field ploughed up in several places, boundary walls pulverised. Northgate, the principal business street, lying at a lower level than the Moor, escaped much serious damage. Happily, too, the railway station, crowded with fugitives, was spared. Majestic old St. Hilda's was holed in the roof, the Baptist Chapel shot through, the Roman Catholic Church of St. Mary's struck. It is not easily explained how so many of the sacred, sculptured symbols of Christian shrines have escaped destruction in France and Belgium, when the buildings containing them have been destroyed. Here, at St. Mary's, the Madonna remained uninjured when the setting was broken away.

The following list includes the places of worship, schools. public institutions and works at Hartlepool that were under shell-fire and more or less damaged:—

St. Hilda's Parish Church.
St. Mary's Roman Catholic Church.
Baptist Chapel.
Carnegie Library.
Cleveland Hall.
Prissick Schools.
Hart Road Schools.
Richardson, Westgarth's Engineering Works.
Cement Works.
Corporation Tram Depôt.
Irvine's Shipyard.

Residential property in Moor Terrace and Victoria Place was well-nigh entirely wrecked. It was in Victoria Terrace that an officer of the Salvation Army, Adjutant William Avery, lost his life. Two sisters, the Misses Kay, were killed in an upper room of their house in Cliff Terrace by a shell fired at the Lighthouse Battery. In this terrace, too, Miss Geipel was so seriously injured that she died a short time afterwards. The tenement house, 30, William Street, was, like No. 2, Wykeham Street, Scarborough, a veritable house of tragedy. The upper part of this house was the home of Mr. and Mrs. Dixon and their six children. Mr. Dixon was away with Kitchener's Army at the time of the bombardment, but his wife and children, seeking to escape from the house, were struck down by an exploding

Showing where Shell came through Ceiling at
Mr. Herbert Humphries' Shop,
92, Lynn Street, West Hartlepool.

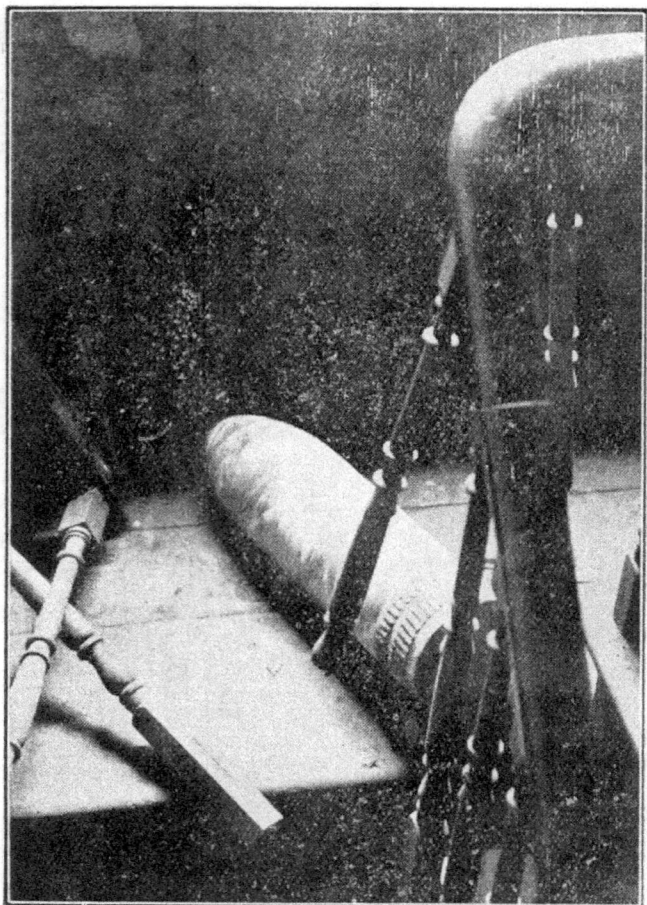

Where Shell finally landed in Mr. Humphries' Shop
without exploding.

shell. The mother was so maimed as to necessitate the amputation of a leg. She was unconscious for some days and is still (February 12) in hospital. Of her children, three were killed and two injured. Mr. Dixon has since been granted a "compassionate discharge" and has returned to his surviving family. John and Peter White-house, two children living in the basement of the same tenement, were killed in the street. At 3, Lilley Street, Charles Cornforth and his two daughters were killed and their mother injured. In these sad instances was the greatest aggregate loss of life in single houses. But all around were harrowing scenes, taxing the nerve and skill of the brave ones who went to the rescue. Here an arm and part of a head had been blown off, here a young woman literally scattered in pieces, a poor woman riddled while gathering sea coal. Two brothers, going to school, were struck with fragments of shell. One was killed outright, the other died soon afterwards. Two daughters of a naval stoker were killed while staying with their grandfather. A shell struck the corner of his house and threw him across the room. On going afterwards to the door to seek his grandchildren he found both lying dead among the dislodged bricks. An old lady of eighty-six was killed by a piece of shell weighing three pounds, which was afterwards taken from her shoulder. A mother, carrying her child, was killed while the child escaped unhurt. These ghastly instances might be multiplied, many cases given where one was taken, the other left. But enough has been said here to show what the ordeal by fire, to which the people of the ancient borough were subjected, was like. These were civilians unprepared, taken by surprise. None knew what to do as the great horror over-took them. "Then shrieked the timid and stood still the brave." Or, save for the crash of the broadsides,

> There was a silence deep as death;
> And the boldest held his breath.

The angel of death had spread his wings on the blast; the smiles of joy had given way to the tears of woe.

From such scenes as these one can imperfectly gather what those on a battleship must be like when masts and turrets, guns and mechanical fittings are swept away by a tornado of shell. On one French village as many as 80,000 shells have been hurled. The bombardment of the East coast, fierce and frightful as it was to those who experienced it, made but little lasting impression on the world outside. It must be accorded its relative position among the lesser incidents of a world-wide war. One war leads to another. The Great War will, in the course of the ages, probably be followed by a greater. Man is mighty in doing, but he excels in undoing. As long as the emotions of hate and fear form part of man's economy, so long as the ambition to subdue others impels some natures forward to the greatest crimes, so long will the world tremble under the scourge of war.

In all (to February 5) 60 individuals were killed at Hartlepool during the bombardment, or have since died from wounds inflicted at the time, and 160 wounded. Of these, nine belonged to the King's Forces. Of the 18th Service Battery of the Durham Light Infantry, a " Pals " Company of lads with three months' training, five were killed as they stood in a group near the Lighthouse Battery, and one has since died of wounds. Of the Durham Royal Garrison Artillery two were killed, and of the Engineer Sappers one. Fifteen people were killed in the streets, six at Richardson and Westgarths, four at Irvine's shipyard, and two at the docks. Of those killed in houses, with the exception of one, all lost their lives in upper rooms.

First Aid for the less seriously injured was given in forty cases by the police, under Chief Constable A. Winterbottom at the Police Station. Dangerous cases were treated at the Hartlepools Hospital, the Workhouse Hospital, and at the Graham Street Military Offices. Never were these institutions under greater strain and stress, never did the surgical staff and nurses show more sympathetic skill under distressing circumstances.

Eighty-five properties were seriously damaged. The loss to owners at an average of £300 each would bring the total amount to £25,500. This may be more or less.

487 claims for indemnification have been sent in through the Corporation, besides those forwarded direct to the Secretary, Bombardment Claims Committee, London.

The churches, the public and private buildings of Hartlepool were, as modern artillery is ranged, so near to the guns of the attacking ships, so prominent in their outlines, that they could not fail to receive the full brunt of the enemy's fire. West Hartlepool, not so easily distinguished in the imperfect light of a hazy December morning, suffered less by comparison. The younger town covers a much larger area, her public buildings and churches are, necessarily, far more numerous for her greater population. Yet, they entirely escaped the rain of shells. A shell burst above the Wesley Church in Victoria Road, but beyond shattering the windows did no further damage. The docks and the shipping in them would, naturally, be pleasing marks for the naval representatives of a hostile nation, whose mercantile marine has been swept from the seas by the British navy. At the moment of the bombardment, shells coming over the breakwater began to fall in the harbour mouth and around the North pier. As they struck the surface huge columns of water rose high in the air like eruptive geysers. The gunners were getting the range. Nearer the shells came to their objective, plunging into the waters of the docks and hitting the ships lying there.

Quite a little tragedy occurred around the Dockmaster's, Capt. C. Nicholson's offices, which happily were spared a direct hit. Shells and shell fragments flew all around and about it, and those who were caught in the storm made haste to find sheltering cover. A group of men, with one woman, twelve in all, had gathered under the lea of the Dockmaster's offices, when a shell hit one of the crab-winches at the dock gates and smashed its stout iron coverlet and parts of the winch fittings beneath into smithereens. Broken shell from the explosion struck down six of the number, including Miss Horsley, the young woman. All, at once received first aid treatment in the mess-room at the hands of Mr. William Kay, in charge of the ambulance, but Miss Horsley died a few minutes after being rescued. So hot was the fire, that a cup Mr. Kay was using for the carriage of water to the wounded was hurled from his hand and shot through in two places, as with the help of a lad he went to Miss Horsley's assistance. A serjeant of the guard and one private were among the wounded, of whom four subsequently died. Mr. Kay, when all others had fled, stuck to his post of duty and of mercy with a splendid heroism worthy of being specially recounted among the great deeds performed by the Ambulance Corps elsewhere in stricken streets.

Exploded shell, from which Mr. Kay so narrowly escaped, struck Mr. Churcher, a Customs officer, as he sought safety in his boat at a corner of the dock. He died two days after. Mr. Oakes, a brother officer was also seriously wounded, and at the moment of writing is still in hospital. In Harbour Terrace a roof was entirely destroyed by shell. Three child inmates were injured, one of whom died. Another shell, after striking the dock wall, rebounded into what is known as the old Tip End. There, a Mr. Wood was killed, and his child, since dead, struck by fragments. The sad case of Mr. Wood's sister-in-law will be recalled to mind. Among many remarkable instances of narrow shell-shaves was that of Captain Hackers. He, with the others, had put the Dockmaster's offices between them and the screeching shell. Yet a fragment from the crab-winch found him out and carried away part of his trouser leg without doing him any injury.

With the shells coming in rapid succession over the breakwater from the north-east, the shipping in the docks was certain to be hit, indeed, with the water in a boil from falling shell and shell-pieces, it was passing strange so much of it remained safe and sound.

> The "City of Newcastle" was damaged in the upper bridge.
>
> A new steamer, "The Firfield," was receiving her engines. A shell went in at No. 1 hold and out at the starboard bow, leaving a jagged hole some three feet in diameter.
>
> The "Sagama River" steamer, a new ship, taking in engines at Irvine's Yard, was shot through amidships and two poor fellows killed in the hold.

The "Ingrid II." was holed through the starboard bow.

The "Munificent" had been carrying troops. Her mess-room steward was killed on board.

The s.s. "Phoebe," lying at Hartlepool, had the second mate killed by a piece of shell which fell on deck.

From this line of fire the N.E.R. Goods Station, in Mainsforth Terrace, was exposed, and two shells apparently fell in the yard, but so far as the rolling-stock was concerned only two box waggons were almost blown away. Illustrations of their wrecked condition, after being under shell-fire, are given in these pages. These waggons were loaded separately, with rope and sweets. The rope, cut up by the exploding shell, was strewn in filmy fibres over the station yard, and looked more like very light tobacco than strands of rope. A shortage of sweets in some shops followed the destruction of the second waggon.

The shear-like cutting power of the exploding shell was well illustrated on the railway line, two pieces of steel rails being cut clean out as with a knife. The ballast was disturbed in places, possibly by fragments, but little damage was done to the bed of the line. One box waggon, standing a few yards from the severed rails, was shot right through in nearly a hundred perforations. A 11-inch unexploded shell was found after the bombardment to have lodged between pit-props at "Slag Island." From one siding near the passenger station a sleeper was dislodged and, blown across the Clarence Road, smashed the ornamental iron gate at "The Willows," and finally rested in the front garden. By the new concrete wall beyond, a telegraph pole was to be seen cut in two and wires entangled and broken for some distance.

Happily, little loss to man or beast occurred at this busy centre. A staff of rolleymen were getting ready for the day's work when a shell fell near them, but did no bodily injury. Few of the clerical staff were about at the time. Pieces of shrapnel were found in the Receiving House, all the windows of which were broken.

Shunter Sarginson received some thirty wounds and died afterwards.

Mooring-boatman, G. Dring, while on duty at West Dock, was killed.

Gatekeeper, A. Wiles, was injured at the Church Square subway to bondyard.

Two deck hands in the employ of the N.E.R. were wounded.

With such a vast quantity of timber stacked in a line with the railway, a fierce and extensive fire from shell exploding among it would not have been surprising. As it was, a great destruction of this principal importation was brought about in the timber sidings of May & Hassell, Thos. Walker & Sons, and Geo. Horsley & Co. In a lesser degree, loss was sustained by R. Wade & Sons and W. Pearson & Co., timber merchants.

Damage to house-property in West Hartlepool was very considerable, and extended over a wide area. Claims for indemnity will probably reach 1,500. Property, more or less wrecked, was to be seen in about 200 streets immediately after the bombardment. Where windows were open, glass was not so much broken, but displaced air from explosions, caused widespread loss in this respect. In the fourth line of fire, the Old Town suffered severely in Dock Street, St. John Street, Knowles Street and Pilot Street, many houses being demolished and many lives sacrificed. Mrs. Moon was found dead in the passage of No. 11, Dover Street, a shell apparently dropping upon the front of her house. Lynn Street, like Church Street, was favoured. A shell passed through the attic of the Ward-Jackson Hotel, and seems to have continued its flight to the opposite side of the street. There, it entered the shop of Mr. Humphries. Mr. W. Ropner had a double dose of German shell-mixture, for not only was "Ambleside," his residence in Elwick Road, damaged and his servant, Miss J. Stoker, killed, but a huge hole was made in the frontage of his offices in Mainsforth Terrace.

Dene Street, opening out on Middleton Road, and Dock Street in the Old Town, were veritable death traps. In May Street, the corner of a house was knocked down. The offices of the Corporation Tram Depot were damaged. Much loss was sustained in Brougham Terrace. The back premises of two houses in Lowthian Road were wrecked. At 171, Alma Street the roof was flicked away, at 172, the bedroom was demolished. The chimney of No. 3, Milton Street, the residence of Mr. Ritchie, was brought down, and went crashing through the roof. A shell went through the roof of the Avenue Road Schools, but did not explode. The roof of No. 6, Lister Street was struck.

A piece of shell was found in the playground of Jesmond Road Schools. In Murray Street, great damage was done to 101 and to the shop premises of Donald Brown & Co., and in Grosvenor Street, Mr. Mustard's first floor room had a straight punch from a 6-inch shell, making a huge gap. In Grange Road, at the residence of Mr. H. C. Crummack, the roof collapsed, and beyond, in Hutton Avenue, Mr. John Hardy's damaged property will not cost much less than £250 to restore and replace. A 6-inch shell broke through the north-east corner of his house. Exploding, it wrecked the billiard room, destroyed pictures, brought down ceilings, cut through doors, made large holes in the walls and broke up the flooring. The billiard table, in framework and covering, was pierced by ninety fragments. Happily, the family were at breakfast below this scene of danger and destruction. The nose of the shell passed through the partition wall into the house of Mr. J. W. Crosby, where it was found. In the same avenue Mr. S. Strover's roof was broken. In accordance with the promise of the Prime Minister that owners and tenants should be indemnified for the loss of property, £25,000 has been allotted to West Hartlepool. Of this sum, £1,500 is for broken windows.

Beyond the material loss resulting from the vicious and sustained fire of the German flotilla upon unarmed, non-combatant towns, the more painful and distressing realities of it were in evidence immediately it had ceased. The first sights that met one's view on venturing into the streets were the prompt ambulance men, under Councillor W. T. Ryan, with stretchers, carrying the maimed and the dying to the several " houses of mercy " already constituted or rapidly improvised for so exceptional and unlooked for an occasion. There they received that sympathetic attention and skill which have made the name of the British surgeon and his nursing staff revered and renowned.

It is only possible to enumerate a few of the more startling instances of the fell morning's work of the German cruisers upon the inhabitants of West Hartlepool. It is quite certain that the health of many persons who were not physically strong, has been permanently injured by shock, and the lives of many more shortened by the terrible ordeal they went through. If proof of this were necessary, it only remains to give the following few pathetic instances of what war means to a thickly-peopled town :—

> At one corner house in Dene Street six or seven persons were immediately killed or died afterwards from wounds received.
>
> Dorothy Caws, 25 years of age, 57, Grosvenor Street, was sitting in an easy chair before the fire when a shell-splinter killed her.
>
> Charles L. C. Ramsey was following his employment as a patternmaker with Richardson, Westgarth & Co., when he was killed.
>
> Thomas Phillips, marker, was found dead in Leeds Street. He had been a victim to shell-fire.
>
> Margaret A. Hunter, 47 years, 11, Bridge Street, was found dead on the sea wall. She had been gathering sea coal.
>
> Rose Owen, 43 years, 1, Pilot Street, was found dead in Pilot Street.
>
> Sarah and Hannah Jobling, 6 years and 4 years, respectively, two sister mites, were found dead in Dock Street.

Moor Terrace Back, Hartlepool.

Victoria Place and Moor Terrace, Hartlepool.

Bridget Corner, 39 years, and Margaret Henighan, 8 years, were both found dead in Dock Street.

Annie Corner, 37 years, 1, Dock Street, had only been confined twelve days previously. She died from shock.

Hilda Horsley, 17 years, was killed in Middleton Road as she was on her way to a situation.

John Staunch, 41 years, was found dead on the sea wall.

Alfred C. B. Claude, a schoolboy of 12 years, was found dead in Alma Street.

Hannah Arnold and Mary Ann Harrison were both killed in crossing a street.

Albert and Stanley Walker, 9 years and 6 years, 14, Turnbull Street, were both killed when walking with their mother.

Eleanor Necysey, 6 months, was killed while being carried in arms.

Nicholas Capeling, 25 years, heater, was struck on passing through the exit of Gray's New Yard.

James Lynett, 42 years, labourer, was killed in Scarborough Street.

Sarah Hodgson, 56 years, 32, Thirlmere Street, was attending to her household duties. A shell burst in the back street and killed her.

Matthew Skelton, 54 years, 82, Balmoral Terrace, was killed. He was an assistant timekeeper in Gray's Old Yard.

Thomasina Scarr, 44 years, 1, Richardson Street, was walking with her daughter in Sandringham Road, when she was pierced by shell.

In all, up to March, 1915, 119 persons, in Hartlepool and West Hartlepool, have died either from the immediate, or after-effects of, shell-fire. The number of these temporarily wounded or permanently maimed is certainly not less than 400.

In Memoriam.

Sleep on, brave hearts! the ebbing tide
  Hath carried you far out from shore,
Yet your frail bark shall safely ride,
    Where seas ne'er toss, nor tempests roar.
      Sleep on!

'Tis night with you, the stars look down;
  But shadows flee where suns ne'er set;
Where smiles ne'er change into a frown,
    Where days pass by without regret,
      Sleep on!

Alone, becalmed, unmoved, sleep sound,
  Nor piping watch, nor pealing bell,
Nor friends that lie with you around,
    Shall wake you from your hallowed spell,
      Sleep on!

Sleep on till golden morning beams,
  Till cloud and mist are lost in light;
Till out of wrong the glad right gleams.
    Till dim-eyed faith be lost in sight,
      Sleep on!

As waves in might, as waves in glee,
  As waters breaking on the shore,
Your seraph voices, pure and free,
    Shall swell for ever, evermore,
      Sleep on!

It would be as wrong to say that the people of the towns
attacked were without emotion, excitement and fear, as to
say they were in a state of panic. The towns, as a whole,
were calm in their inherent strength. But the sudden
concussion and vibration were as though an earthquake or
an avalanche had, with a violent suddenness, been launched
upon them. Many indeed set out for their day's work, or
went on with it, if begun, with outward indifference. But
to the great majority there must have been a feeling of
fearful, anxious, intense foreboding. Especially must this
have been the case where mothers with their young families

were concerned. It must have aroused an inward sense akin to that experienced by a young soldier going, for the first time, under fire.

Many, indeed, broke loose from their home-fortresses to seek safety in the streets, in the companionship of their neighbours, in the country outside. Considerable numbers hurried to the railway stations to get away in haste from what, at the moment, seemed to them impending ruin. They had read, and now seen, what German kultur, in its maddest moments of expression, meant.

Soon after the guns opened fire and it was realised that the gifted Huns had indeed descended upon the coast, steps were taken by those in authority to calm the minds of the people and to restore confidence. In West Hartlepool the majority of the 400 special constables, organised under the control of the Borough War Emergency Committee, were on duty in every part of the town. By their assistance and advice they rendered excellent service among the most distracted and unnerved. On the cessation of the cannonade, drafts of these constables, on foot and on cycles, were despatched to the outlying country to persuade the fugitives that there was no further cause for alarm, and to induce them to return to their homes. Many had indeed left their garments and fled. Many would not be comforted, nor did they return till nightfall. Numbers were, however, reconciled, and came back upon the advice given.

Whilst the bombardment was still going on, the Mayor of West Hartlepool, Councillor J. R. Fryer, summoned the War Emergency Committee to meet him and the Superintendent of Police, Mr. T. McDonald, at the Police Office. This Committee included Alderman and Major R. Martin, V.D., and Councillors W. J. Coates, W. T. Ryan, J. W. Boanson, W. Edgar, T. F. Thompson, E. O. Bennett, and the Borough Engineer, Mr. Nelson F. Dennis. The following proclamation was thereupon drawn up and issued to the town :—

PROCLAMATION.

NAVAL BOMBARDMENT.

The Civil Population are requested, as far as possible, to keep to their houses for the present. The situation is now secure.

The Group Leaders of each Ward will advise in case of further danger.

Any unexploded shells must not be touched, but information as to the position thereof given to the nearest Police Officer, or to the Police Station.

J. R. FRYER,

Mayor.

Dated the 16th day of December, 1914.

GOD SAVE THE KING.

This timely and prudent step did much towards reassuring the population.

Not perhaps till the day following the bombardment did the people of the port even begin to realise all the possibilities of being for forty minutes under the shell-fire of modern naval guns. Dotted here and there along the lines of fire were, however, startling evidences of the tempest that had overshadowed them. Here and there, on doorstep and pavement, were pools and splashes of blood. Here a peaceful home had been brought bodily down and remained to tell its story as a heap of tangled wreckage; there, a family group had fallen as on a battlefield, some with their last smile, some maimed, mangled, broken.

Can there be surprise at a prevailing state of high nervous tension? Is it to be wondered at that many were mentally unhinged, that others should, one by one, drop out of the ranks, victims of shock? Whilst in this unbalanced state worse was to come. On Friday morning the following notice was issued to the public through the Post Office :—

Telegraph message from Staff-Captain Lyons, Head-quarters, Hartlepool, December 18, 1914: "Received message to look out for hostile airship. Warn all constables to warn all residents on approach of airship to go into basements of their homes and remain till danger is past. Advise them to keep cool, and not congregate in groups in streets. Rumours may be false, but everyone to be prepared."

The special constables were again called together. Instructions were given them to apprise the people of the possibility of a new danger being on the way and how best to meet it. Ill news travels fast and gathers worse import on its journey. Somehow, Captain Lyons' poster was misread and misinterpreted. Word went round that the German ships were again in the bay and about to renew their attack. This was straining distracted minds to the breaking-point. An industrial section of 70,000 souls threw down its tools, hurrying away, anywhere, from the German wrath to come. This was the saddest day in the town's history. Again, the morning was only half-awake. Mothers snatched hold of their children and raced for the Park, the byways and hedges. The staff at the railway station could hardly cope with the rush for the trains. At York, on the evening of this sorrow-strewn day, would-be passengers to the Hartlepools were told that it was doubtful if they would get through.

The mischief had been sown broadcast; the harm was done. A second proclamation was issued by the Mayor in the afternoon. It stated that a misunderstanding of Captain Lyons' notice had unfortunately arisen. It expressed a hope that all would go on with the "daily round," for there was no cause for alarm. It was too late. Many families who left the town that day have not yet returned. The guns brought silent apprehension in their roar, the distorted message rang the alarm bells far and wide.

When the unfortunate scare was at its worst and people were in flight as if for their lives, motor-cyclists were sent into the country beyond the town to induce these terror-stricken ones to return to their homes.

It was pitiful to see mothers and children half-clad, some without boots, carrying parcels of food and clothing hastily put together, in fear and trembling. Many of these fugitives were overtaken eight miles away and it was difficult to reassure them.

AMBULANCE WORK.

During the bombardment and throughout the distracted and distressing hours that followed, the police, under Superintendent T. McDonald, gave most valuable help in ambulance work, and in an endeavour to maintain the ordinary quiet and collected behaviour of the town.

Ten minutes after the guns had announced their arrival, motor cyclists, under the direction of Mr. W. T. Walton (Transport Officer), were out on rescue work. Augmented by cars, which were rushed by their owners to co-operate with them, not a moment was lost in conveying the injured to the hospitals and relief centres. Serious cases were thus enabled to benefit by immediate surgical treatment.

Among the foremost in this speedy help, some of it bravely given under shell fire, were Mr. J. G. Robson, Mr. P. Scott, Mr. W. Meredith, Mr. T. Brooks and Mr. A. Hyde. The motor cyclists had received instructions to be immediately on their way should emergency arise, and within a few minutes of the attack, Mr. E. M. Tweddle, Mr. E. Forslind, Mr. J. Charlesworth and Mr. E. Wright were on their machines prepared to carry out the instructions of the Military. Many of them had narrow escapes. For the ten days following the bombardment they were still active where duty called. Much praise and gratitude is due to them for the unflinching way in which they went on these errands of mercy. With the telegraph wires severed or down between the Hartlepools, additional responsibility was theirs in conveying telegrams from the old borough to the new.

Since that day of assault and battery the service of motor cars and motor cycles has been effectively developed and is now an efficient organization recognised by the War Office.

VII.

RETROSPECTIVE AND REFLECTIVE.

For nought so vile that on the earth doth live,
But to the earth some special good doth give;
Nor aught so good, but, strained from that fair use,
Revolts from true birth, stumbling on abuse.

Romeo and Juliet.

To be under shell-fire is, happily, not a common experience.
A taste for it has yet to be acquired. Until the ,East
coast was brought within striking distance by battle cruisers
having the speed of an ordinary train, and by explosive
shell rendered capable of hitting its mark at ten miles,
scientific progress in the art of killing and maiming had
been read about, but could rarely have been actually seen.
It is the unexpected that happens. When it comes in the
guise of German shell, we are pulled up with a sudden
jolt that tries every mainspring in our bodily mechanism.
We may not have lost our ordinary courage, but the shock
to our insular pride and our insular characteristics is so
great that we are dazed by the blow and altogether lose
our bearings. Perhaps we stand still in anxious listening,
yet without ordered thought; quite possibly we run hither
and thither having no object in view, no goal towards which
we would be making. As in a dream, our thoughts run
riot, or our nerves are entirely cut off from their head
power-station. We had heard that there might be raids,
but we gave no heed to tales of approaching invasion. We
had lived in our little paradise so long without molestation,
that we regarded its fruit as not only forbidden, but beyond
the reach of another to gather. We had looked upon
ourselves, as not only secure in our freedom, but unassail-
able in our island-fortress. Half of our countrymen,
notwithstanding all that has befallen our neighbours, live
on day after day in a like self-satisfied persuasion.

Kitchener's army, some part of it, marches by with a "right, left, right, left" under the window every morning, or breaks camp some evening for the Channel crossing, but the inward peace of these contented ones is not disturbed; sorrow at parting may endure for the night, but joy is with them again in the morning. Perhaps it is well that it should be so. If we lost faith our hopes for the future would be shattered.

The raid startled the East coast to a knowledge of what might be. What do the German people dread more than anything else? Is it not invasion of their own territory? They are the doers, and therefore the witnesses, of all the shameless ruin that ambition, greed and arrogance have brought to the homes of France, Poland and Belgium. They care not. It is their creed that the strong, with a brutal strength and ruthlessness only theirs, shall inherit the land. But none of the misery they have inflicted upon others must bring one tear to the eyes of the Fatherland. Every day their armed conscripts camp amid the wilful waste and wanton destruction of a hideous war. But this must not come nigh them. If it did, all their idols would be shattered, Kaiser and Junker would be no more. The coast raid was to show us what punishment the "mailed fist" could deal out with only a jabbing blow. In that way it was a useful lesson. If a sluggish apathy prevailed, it roused us from it. It made us look things straight in the face. It showed us that a determined enemy could find a way over. It taught us that if a nation valued its inheritance, it must do something more than make haste to be rich, it must make haste to be strong. And it brought out those finer qualities of human sympathy and practical help, which lift men above a common horizon and enable them to pierce the deep blue of a great beyond.

We must give the East coast raid not more than its due proportion in the great maelstrom of a whirling war. We must apportion it its relative position among things vast, and terrible in their consequences. To those who suffered from it, it seemed the greatest calamity of their lives.

Dene Street, West Hartlepool.

Sussex Street, Hartlepool.

So perhaps it was. One was taken, the other left. In some few cases hardly that one was left. And yet, by comparison, it was only a small thing. Those who lived away from the sound of it sympathised without doubt. It brought consternation that such a thing could be. But it was soon forgotten. Every day that followed had other moving pictures of a more vivid intensity. What was a scatterbrained bombardment of forty minutes! What were 1,500 shells to the deluge from a thousand guns! What were 120 lives to the million which have gone home! All precious; but what are they amongst so many? What is the wreckage of a few hundred houses and buildings to the shorn lands and famished faces of a whole country! Those who are gone can only in memory be recalled. They died in Britain's battle. But the material loss can soon be made good. Elsewhere, hardly another generation will see the shell-holes mortared up, the trenches smoothed out, the streets laughing with the good cheer of honest labour. Full of fear and trembling as it was, we must give the raid its true perspective.

It is difficult beyond solution how to understand the mental attitude of Germany in the position she has taken up as arbiter of the destinies of her neighbours, if not of the rest of mankind. How, as it were, to penetrate her inmost soul to discover how it is she thinks and acts in opposition. Here we have a dual personality, the one intellectually fitted to build up, the other, just as mentally strong, equipped from a soldier's button to a sailor's battle-ship, to break down. If we recognise that the Germans are a martial people, versed as perhaps no other in the arts of war, we must concede at the same time that, for nearly half a century, she has been diligent in, and devoted to, what we term the arts of peace. She had made herself industrially strong. Scientifically, she was abreast of all other competitors. She bid fair to capture the markets of the world. "Made in Germany" was a passport to the small purchaser and the great buyer in all lands, not excepting our own. She had grown in wealth, knowledge

and power. She had acquired colonial possessions and had
built the finest mercantile fleets. She had learnt how to
concentrate her efforts on any single object. To be a
German was to be thorough and alas! also to be "frightful."

We, like Germany, have placed a great deal of our money
on education. It was to carry us along the track leading
to a greater, yet a higher type of national prosperity. It
was to break down the walls of "class," to ensure an
equality of opportunity. We had so persuaded ourselves
of a future peaceful career as to give up preparations for
war. Germany, studded with universities, had come to be
regarded, by at least one British statesman, as his "spiritual
home." In her methods of education she had gone beyond
us. She had systematised, organized, tabulated, with the
precision of the most finely-balanced clockwork. She had
numbered every skilled workman for the immediate
necessities of the State. In our social legislation we had
taken the groundwork of her plans. We had introduced
her methods to our schools. We sent our children to
Germany for their higher education. Truly, these Germans
are a wonderful people.

But the real soul of Germany inhabited quite a different
body. It was the spirit of "force" that really inspired
and moved her. "Force" to her was the only remedy.
"Force," unscrupulous, tyrannical force, was her actual
spiritual adviser. It was everywhere present as the demon
of mischief. To stamp the German signature on every
corpuscle of other men's blood, so that it should flow through
and permeate all corporate systems, was the Teutonic ideal.
That was German "kultur." To capture the trade of the
world, to command the seas, to conquer the strong, to
intimidate or annihilate the weak was the real higher
education lisped at the cradle, continued to the grave. It
was the gospel of the philosophers. The aristocratic
Junkers would have no other; the people, as a whole,
received it gladly. The one half of the German was living
in the Stone Age, the other half in the age of electricity
and steel. The one half was savage, the other half civilised.

But always the barbarian was the driving power. The religion taught was the religion of war. Not war by the few for the many, but war in which every man, woman and child put every ounce of strength, every penny that "force" might prevail. One cannot understand this soul of Germany, this mental attitude, this paradox. A part is cut away from the good to make the evil stronger. The East coast raid was a hint to us of what "Force," when applied by the full-striking power of sixty-eight millions of Germans, would really mean to us. It was an object-lesson we should do well not to forget.

War is the world's greatest woe. It should be man's last resource to save himself. Except that war was always necessary to Germany, there was nothing to provoke her to the Great War. It was not her last resource, but perhaps it was ours. Ours, in this way. We were, politically, run mad. The Party virus had poisoned our blood. We were ready to sacrifice all national aspirations for good to the shrine of political expediency. We were just on the brink of a national catastrophe, riding straight for a fall. The middle class mind was centred on one object, how to get rich in the least possible time. It was every man for himself and the devil for the hindmost. The richer were getting richer by the poor being made the poorer. We were socially unsound. Germany knew it, and had long persuaded herself that she was the rightful, the only possible heir, to our world-wide estate. The righteous taketh it by force. To Germany, this force was the mechanism of war. She was the "righteous." The Great War has saved us from ourselves. We have to pay the price in lives and treasure, but it cannot leave us as we were. If it cannot make us young again, it can and will leave us older in wisdom. It will leave us chastened in spirit, ennobled in adversity. It will give us another long lease of life. It will physically and morally strengthen us. War is not all red; interwoven with it are strands of white.

Two questions are uppermost in the minds of millions. They are repeated daily in these islands, in the homes of our allies, in all the countries of neutral peoples, in all places where civilised mankind gathers together. It is proof, if indeed proof were needed, how the whole earth trembles, asleep and awake, at the shock of such tremendous battle. This world-conflict will leave its scars on the face of Europe for many generations, its heavy finger long on the pulse of the great human family. The first question is, "How long will the war last?" He would be a bold prophet who would definitely place a limit to its duration. It seems too gigantic, too abnormal to have a lengthened existence. Were it to go on for many years the most physically fit of the male populations of the several countries engaged would be practically wiped out. The results would be disastrous. The weak, if not the meek, would then inherit the despoiled earth. The cost of it spells bankruptcy in every day's reckoning. It is carried on at such high pressure that the human machine somewhere is bound presently to crack. 'Tis a question of endurance under a heartbreaking strain.

Germany had reckoned on a short war, speedy and triumphant. The success of 1870 had inspired her with the belief that a second breathless march through France to the gates of Paris would leave her in possession, the while she settled her account with Russia. Belgium brought her up, Britain and France set her face homewards. Can she again go forwards? It seems impossible. But so long as the German people cling to the doctrine of "force," the effort to do so will no doubt be repeated. But there are signs that the great rush has spent itself. When the greatest of Continental military powers stoops to petty, inhuman methods to attain the goal she aims at, the end may be nearer than we think. When a boxer hits below the belt, he is hoping that a foul blow will effect what a manly one couldn't. The raids upon the East coast, the dropping of bombs upon unarmed Norfolk, the sowing broadcast of mines, the savage treatment of British prisoners of war, the destruction of neutral ships are all signs of weakness, even if they follow the cult of "frightfulness." "Frightfulness," itself, is evidence of a cowardly incapacity. The teaching of the war-lords and philosophy-professors has increased the hunger for loot, but it has demoralised the German soldier and the German people.

And the second question asked is, "Will this war be the last?" We have been disillusioned. We more than dreamt of the brotherhood of nations. Wars would cease because the main army would refuse to fight. The workers would join hands across the seas and turn their swords into ploughshares. But our Socialist German brothers rushed as eagerly into the fray as the most pronounced sword-rattler. Obedience is made strong in discipline. The love of country comes before all other ideals. If the German people will throw over their cherished idols of "force" and "frightfulness" and the advocates of them, if they will renounce ideas of tramping over the earth in victorious martial array, if they will let little men live to teach them how truly to become great, if they will subdue their brutal arrogance, the world will be quick to recognise their reformed character, and then the Great War will result in a Great Peace. But only when this warring world shall dissolve will there be a void in the universe where conflict, where Hate, with aught else, can no longer find place.

BOMBARDMENT OF THE PORT OF HARTLEPOOL.
DECEMBER 16, 1914.

ITS ANNUAL COMMEMORATION AS A THANKOFFERING DAY.

"Under Shell-Fire" having reached a second edition, it was thought that further demands for it would cease. That, however, is not so. From all parts of the country inquiries and requests respecting it have been made. To comply with these, this third edition has been issued. Incidents connected with the historic bombardment of the two Hartlepools are continually being recalled. To include these has been the aim of the author with the hope of still further completing the record of an event which cannot be forgotten by the present inhabitants, nor fail to be recalled by future generations so long as we as a nation shall imperially exist.

The nimble wit of Councillor J. W. Boanson was never more in evidence than in his suggestion, among many others, to the Hospital Buttonhole Saturday Committees that each recurring anniversary of the bombardment should stand apart as a special "Flag Day," when thanksgiving offerings might be made to the Hartlepool and Cameron Hospitals by those who had escaped a deadly peril. This suggestion was the outcome of a happy thought, and received immediate and general support. Never during their existence had these great and merciful institutions been so full to overflowing as on this day of German warlike invasion of our bordering sea. Never before had there been seen in them so many appealing faces, so many torn and suffering human forms. And never was there a more willing, ready, eager rush to aid and to save than that of the physicians, surgeons, ambulances and nurses of the two towns. With all the horrors of a battle-field around them, they neither quailed nor failed in their noble endeavour.

COUNCILLOR HARRY SALMON.
President and Chairman Thankoffering Organization.

COUNCILLOR J. W. BOANSON,
Originator of Bombardment Thanksgiving Day.

Thankoffering Day must always be lettered in heavy type, must always be marked out by a date which, to the Hartlepools, will distinguish it from all others.

To accentuate this, to supplement in some measure the efforts of those who, year by year, appeal to a sympathising people, this third edition of "Under Shell-Fire" is offered to the public as a souvenir of a memorable, if terrible awakening of the Port, and a reminder also of the splendidly successful efforts of those who have organised and carried through with forethought and skill the great scheme for the immediate help and permanent support of the two hospitals.

Thanksgiving Day has been fortunate in enlisting for its annual effort a happy band of brothers, comrades in arms of peace and of mercy. Notably among these stands out Councillor Harry Salmon as Life President of the organization called into being to keep and perpetuate it. His ability as a leader and organiser has stood the test. Success has been followed by even greater success as time hastens on, as the noise of guns, as the bursting of bombs, as the shouts and the cries of husband, brother, son—the bravest of British braves—proclaim amidst hideous ruin and an agony prolonged that the end is not yet.

The beginnings and development of a movement such as this constitute a record all its own and worthy of preservation. It will be added to as year follows year and as the Hartlepool and Cameron Hospital continue their work of succour and of healing.

Councillor J. W. Boanson, following up the initial proposal, further suggested that the nett proceeds of Thanksgiving Day should be divided equally between the Hartlepools Hospital and the Cameron Hospital. Beyond this, he was in favour of approaching Councillor Harry Salmon and his successful "Flag Days" Committee with the view of securing their joint co-operation in the larger venture. These proposals were cordially approved and carried. Councillor Salmon was unanimously elected Chairman of the Joint Committees, thereupon expressing his willingness to complete the work of organization and make the necessary arrangements for its practical outcome.

As preliminary steps, a design for a flag and medallion was made by Mr. C. F. Burton and an appeal for subscriptions launched by the Chairman and Councillor T. F. Thompson. Subsequently, lady workers were called in to sell flags and medallions in the streets on "Flag" Day.

Various raffles were taken in hand by members of the Committee, the most successful being "Xmas Cheer" (Mr. E. D. Barker), "Painting" (Coun. J. W. Boanson), "Chair" (Messrs. J. H. Burton and J. Witty), "Bureau" (Messrs. R. H. Hodgson and H. Boothroyd).

December the 18th, 1915, was the nearest Saturday to the bombardment anniversary, and on that day "Flag Day" was held. The lady workers rejoiced in an extremely busy time. Amongst the attractions of the day were a football match between the R.N.A.S. and R.F.C.; members of the Committee in costume making collections; boys made up as shells; side shows; concert party (C. Smith's). In addition, the Birikini Society gave performances and the takings at the Town Hall and the Palladium, Hartlepool, went to augment the funds. One of the most successful attractions was the "War Trophies" exhibition, at which various implements and weapons of war were shown. Included among these were a German gun, lent by the Military, and many forbidding relic reminders of the bombardment. By kind permission of the proprietors of the Empire Theatre, a lecture, by Mr. William Le Quex, was given on Sunday evening, December 19, on the German Spy System. Both financially and instructively it proved most successful. On this evening, too, boxes were placed at the various churches and chapels and the retiring collections made a substantial addition to the general receipts.

Altogether, everything went with a rush of enthusiasm under a most effective organization. The nett result was the splendid sum of £2,048/3/0. Of this amount, £1,048/3/0 was equally divided between the two hospitals, thus clearing them of debt. The balance of £1,000 was handed to the Hartlepools Joint Hospital Trust Fund, the origin of which emanated from Mr. William Cresswell Gray (now

Sir William Cresswell Gray, Bart.). The Trust funds accumulating from this conception have always been equally shared by the two institutions.

In 1916, the "War Charities" Act came into force, and Councillor Salmon's committee was then constituted on business lines and registered under the title of "The Thankoffering Organization." Appended here is the list, which includes Patron, President and Committee:—

THE THANKOFFERING ORGANIZATION.

Patron—

Sir WM. C. GRAY, Bart.

Life-President—

Councillor HARRY SALMON.

Committee—

Coun. J. W. Boanson.	Mr. J. Crawl.	Mr. J. Prideaux.
„ W. Edgar.	„ H. W. Day.	„ B. Proud.
„ W. E. Robinson.	„ J. Dick.	„ J. N. Reid.
„ T. F. Thompson.	„ F. Forster.	„ R. Robinson.
„ J. Urwin.	„ A. Hardy.	„ R. A. Roskell.
Mr. O. Aarvold.	„ R. H. Hodgson.	„ T. R. G. Rowland.
„ J. Atkinson.	„ P. G. Hodgson.	„ R. Stonehouse.
„ E. D. Barker.	„ F. W. Hunter.	„ N. Todd.
„ A. E. S. Barker.	„ A. G. Jesseman.	„ C. S. Wahlstrand.
„ H. Boothroyd.	„ T. Knight.	„ W. Wallace.
„ H. Booton.	„ G. Kitson.	„ T. H. Warwick.
„ J. Broady.	„ H. B. Olsen.	„ F. Witty.
„ H. S. Brymer.	„ S. Pearson.	„ C. S. Woodiwis.
„ J. H. Burton.	„ P. F. Perry.	„ A. Warr.
„ C. F. Burton.	„ J. Proud.	

Hon. Auditor: Mr. T. H. WARWICK.

Hon. Treasurer: Mr. R. H. HODGSON.

Hon. Secretaries: Mr. J. WITTY and Mr. A. E. BAKER.

At the special request of the Buttonhole Saturday Committee, the Thanksgiving Organization carried out the arrangements for "Flag Day" on December 16, 1916, entirely at their own discretion. The routine was similar to that of 1915, with a few exceptions and additions to the programme. In lieu of several smaller raffles, one large drawing was arranged for. This was termed "Xmas Cheer." Carried through by Messrs. E. D. Barker, J. Proud and F. Witty, its success exceeded the hopes of the most sanguine. Not least among the innovations for this anniversary day was a most refreshing performance by the "Dainty Dots" of Miss Susie Lee. Teacher and pupils excelled themselves. This attraction at the Electric Theatre, kindly placed at the disposal of the Committee for the occasion, proved most popular and remunerative, and we shall hope to look forward to its repeatal. The football match, R.N.A.S. v. R.F.C., again delighted a large crowd. An anonymous donor, instead of a monetary contribution, presented a valuable bedroom suite. This was drawn for and made a further handsome addition to the funds.

In the aggregate, the nett result for 1916 exceeded that of 1915 by £311/2/1, the amount at the actual disposal of the Committee after meeting expenses being £2,359/5/1. Of this total, £359/5/1 was equally shared by the two hospitals as in the preceding year. The balance of £2,000 went as an addition to the Trust Fund. For this anniversary a medallion of new design came from Mr. C. F. Burton.

In this year, 1917, "Flag Day" will again be held in December. With the efforts of the Committee, seconded by the support of a generous public, the hope is that the record of 1916 will be equalled, if not exceeded.

Incidentally, it may be mentioned that Councillor Salmon's Committee, now the Thankoffering Organization, have been instrumental in handing over the following amounts to War Charities:—

		£	s.	d.
May, 1915—Serbian Day		1408	14	1
Aug. „ —French Day		1346	12	2
Dec. „ —1st Bombardment Day		2048	3	0
Jan., 1916—V.A.D., West Hartlepool		100	0	0
May —All British Day—				
British Red Cross ... £1068 3 0				
Y.M.C.A. ... 1018 2 9				
R.S.P.C.A. (Army				
Horses) ... 509 1 6—2595		2595	7	3
Nov. —Anglo-Russian Cot		530	0	0
Red Cross Overseas		238	7	2
Dec. „ —2nd Bombardment Day		2359	5	1
Jan., 1917—Sailors' Day		510	0	0
Feb. „ —Military Night (Mayoress' Comforts				
Fund)		145	0	0
April „ —Local Soldiers' Comforts Fund		74	3	9
May „ — „ „ „ ...		62	2	11
June „ —Green Howards (Prisoners of War Fund)		200	0	0
July „ —Red Cross—				
British £1000 0 0				
French ... 330 0 0—1330		1330	0	0

£12,947 15 5

This magnificent sum total gives all-round proof of generous public sympathy and support and emphasises what has already been said of the untiring energy of the man at the wheel and of the singleness of purpose animating the staff of willing workers—Committee and lady helpers—who co-operated with him.

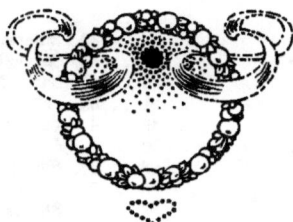

APPENDIX.

LIST OF KILLED AT HARTLEPOOL.

SOLDIERS.

Corporal Liddle, 18th Batt., Durham L.I.
Lance-Corporal Clark „ „
Private T. Jones „ „
  „ L. Turner „ „
  „ W. Rogers „ „
  „ T. Minks „ „
Gunner Houston, Durham R.G.A.
  „ Spence, Durham R.G.A.
Sapper Little, Durham Royal Engineers.

	Age	Residence
Allen, Annie	25	14, Victoria Place.
Ambrose, Robert Lumley ...	33	65, Everard Street.
Ashcroft, Edwin	29	19, Penrith Street.
Avery, William Gordon	49	7, Victoria Place.
Backham, Cuthbert John ...	42	Darlington Terr., West H'pool.
Binns, Samuel	68	21, Ramsey Street, West H'pool.
Bunter, James	32	13, Commercial Street, Middleton.
Chappell, William	15	18, Slake Terrace, Middleton.
Churcher, William Hubert ...	26	29, Clarendon Rd., West H'pool.
Clark, John ...	54	5, Kinburn Street.
Clarke, Charles Stephen	25	47, Sheriff Street, West H'pool.
Cornforth, Charles ...	63	3, Lilly Street.
Cornforth, Polly ...	23	„ „
Cornforth, Jane Ann	17	2, Lilly Street.
Cox, Thomas Garbutt	26	2, Durham Street.
Corner, Annie	37	1, Dock Street.
Cook, James ...	37	28, Rokeby Street.
Crake, John William	15	19, Woods Street.
Cressy, Albert Edwin	29	48, Turnbull Street, West H'pool.
Dixon, George Edward	14	30, William Street.
Dixon, Margaret Ellen	8	„ „
Dixon, Albert	7	„ „
Dring, George	47	30, Elliott Street, West H'pool.
Evans, John	32	30, Charlotte St., West H'pool.
Geipel, Ethel Mary ...	36	17, Cliffe Terrace.
Hamilton, Jessie ...	21	50, Malton Street.
Harper, Elizabeth Agnes	49	4, Moor Terrace.
Harris, Etta ...	30	"Ivyholm," South Crescent.
Healey, John	63	18, Hart Street.
Herbert, Selina	3	5, William Street.
Hodgson, John ...	62	58, Stephenson Street.
Houston, William Stephen ...	22	75, Union Road.
Hudson, Charles William	21	43, Mary Street.

	Age	Residence
Jones, Theophilus	29	44, Ashgrove Av., West H'pool.
Kay, Annie Mabel	34	"Rockside," Cliffe Terrace.
Kay, Florence Josephine	32	,, ,,
Lee, Clementina	25	6, Victoria Place.
Leighton, James Shepherd	56	16, Clifton Street.
Liddle, Alix Oliffe	25	Lindon Avenue, Darlington.
Little, Samuel	20	8, Clyde Street, Jarrow.
Marshall, Catherine	86	41, Mary Street.
Measor, Christopher	10	11, Well's Yard.
Minks, Thomas	25	Melbourne House, Rowlands Gill.
Pearson, John William	25	(s.s. Phoebe), of Robin Hood's Bay.
Ramsey, Charles Leonard Clayton	37	24, Osborne Road, West H'pool.
Redshaw, Margaret Ann	47	50, Watson Street.
Rogers, Walter	25	South View, Bishop Auckland.
Spence, Robert	22	19, Prissick Street.
Stewart, Stanley	6	20, William Street.
Stringer, Ethel	12	10, William Street.
Sullivan, Daniel	47	3, Harrison Street, West H'pool.
Theaker, Richard	23	63, Turnbull Street, West H'pool.
Turner, Leslie Dobson	23	Dalmeny House, Rowlands Gill.
Unthank, Frank	14	24, Woods Street.
Watson, Mary Elizabeth	40	164, Hart Road, Hartlepool.
Wainwright, Freda	19	10, Henry Street.
Watt, Amy	22	2, Marine Crescent.
Whitecross, Peter	8	34, William Street.
Whitecross, John Matthew	6	,, ,,
Williams, Ivy	31	8, Beaconsfield Square.
Woods, Samuel Norman	19	18, Lumley Street.
Wright, William	51	4, Crook Street.
Young, Bertie	13	7, Princess Street, Middleton.

LIST OF KILLED AT WEST HARTLEPOOL.

	Age	Residence
Arnold, Hannah (Mrs.)	33	48, Gas Street.
Asquith, William	51	22, Town Wall, Hartlepool.
Austrin, Beart Beaumont	33	3, May Street.
Bell, Henry Stephen	11	31, Belk Street.
Brennen, Margaret (Mrs.)	52	53, Belk Street.
Brookbanks, Charles Abraham	35	4, Fawcett Street.
Burgon, Robert	38	7, Mill Street.
Capeling, Nicholas	25	4, Darlington St., Hartlepool.
Caws, Dorothy	25	57, Grosvenor Street.
Claude, Alfred Camille Benard	12	11, Gordon Street.
Cook, Robert Wilfred	8	40, Turnbull Street.
Cook, Harold	10	,, ,,

	Age	Reside ce
Cooper, Edward ...	... 16 ...	2, Exeter Street.
Corner, Bridget (Mrs.)	... 39 ...	4, Dock Street.
Frankland, Catherine	4 ...	3, Leeds Street.
Gray, Wiliam	... 23 ...	3, Ballast Hill, Blyth.
Harrison, Mary Ann (Mrs.)	... 60 ...	24, Dene Street.
Henderson, Joseph ...	... 47 ...	45, Turnbul Street.
Hen'ghan, Margaret	8 ...	18, Dock Street.
Heslop, Thomas	7 ...	19, Brafferton Street.
Highan, Thomas ...	... 11 ...	9, Henry Street, Hartlepool.
Hodgeor, Sarah (Mrs.)	... 56 ...	32, Thirlmere Street.
Hodgeon, William ...	... 43 ...	9, Water Street.
Horsley, Hilda	... 17 ...	9, Wood Street, Hartlepool.
Hunter, Margaret Ann (Mrs.)	... 47 ...	11, Bridge Street.
Hunter, Samuel Hall	... 16 ...	1, Alexander Terrace, Hart Lane.
Jackson, Edith (Mrs.)	... 39 ...	49, Perth Street.
Jacobs, Joseph ...	... 13 ...	32, Belk Street.
Jobling, Sarah	6 ...	22, South Street.
Jobling, Hannah ...	4 ...	„ „
Lofthouse, Benjam'n	7 months,	25, Belk Street.
Lynett, James	... 42 ...	11, Staindrop Street.
McGuire, John	... 15 ...	58, Cameron Road.
Moon, Julia (Mrs.) ...	... 68 ...	11, Dover Street.
Mossom, Thomas	... 55 ...	2, St. John Street.
Necysey, Eleanor	6 months,	2, Pilot Street.
Owen, Rose (Mrs.) ...	... 43 ...	1a, Pilot Street.
Owen, Mary Ellen ...	... 17	„ „
Peart, Wiliam	5 ...	30, Turnbull Street.
Peart, Charles	2 ...	„ „
Phillips, Thomas ...	... 16 ...	2, Leeds Street.
Reybould, Hannah (Mrs.)	... 36 ...	37, Darlington Terrace.
Sarginson, William	... 22 ...	67, Beechwood Road.
Scarr, Thomasina (Mrs.)	... 44 ...	1, Richardson Street.
Simmons, Stanley ...	5 ...	22, Campion Street.
Skelton, Matthew	... 54 ...	82, Studley Road.
Staunch, John	... 41 ...	44, Alliance St., Hartlepool.
Stoker, Jane ...	... 41 ...	" Ambleside," West Hartlepool.
Swales, Matthew H.	... 36 ...	21, Croft Terrace, Hartlepool.
Walker, Albert	9 ...	14, Turnbull Street.
Walker, Stanley ...	6 ...	„ „
Wheelwright, Bewick ...	... 15 ...	15, South Street.
Wilkinson, Laura Annie Harrison	... 12 ...	20, Dene Street.
Witty, Stanley ...	... 10 ...	27, Belk Street.
Woods, Josiah ...	... 36 ...	6, Harbour Terrace.
Woods, Martha Jane	6 ...	„ „

The Jury's verdict in most cases was:—

"Killed in time of war by shells fired from German warships off the coast of the Hartlepools."

LIST OF ILLUSTRATIONS.

For the illustrations in this book photographs were most kindly lent by the following : C. Brittain, S. W. Bell, W. Railton, A. H. Barrett, West Hartlepool ; A. Price, Hartlepool ; E. T. W. Dennis and Sons, Scarborough. To them the author tenders his sincere thanks.

HARTLEPOOL
WAR EMERGENCY COMMITTEE.

At Hartlepool, the special constables, of whom the greater majority are members of the Citizens' Training League, worked in conjunction with the League, and it is impossible to give the names separately.

Commandant Citizens' Training League—Mr. C. I. SMYTH, J.P.
Group Leader, South Ward—Councillor J. FIRBY.
    ,,   North Ward—Councillor G. WILLIAMSON.
    ,,   Throston Ward—Mr. H. RIDING.
    ,,   Middleton Ward—Councillor W. O. ATKINSON.
Chief Constable A. WINTERBOTTOM, Hon. Secretary.

Abram Barnett.	W. W. Maddams.	John G. Denton.
Edw. Hubbard.	Alf. E. Woodhead.	John Nelson.
Ernest W. Blakey.	Wm. P. Scott.	Geo. E. Pallett.
Thos. P. Harbron.	J. V. Walton.	Thos. Maynard.
Chas. Charlton.	Alf E. Bradford.	John W. Woodrup.
Richard Waterman.	Arthur Peacock.	Cuthbert Pounder.
Jas. Pattison.	Fred Shaw.	Thos. S. Little.
Arthur H. Cox.	Thos. R. Bell.	Geo. Jackson.
Hy. Cappleman.	Geo. Clark.	Robt. H. Holman.
Frank P. Horsley.	Ralph Orde.	Hy. Nicholson.
Alex Duff.	John T. Miller.	Frank Legg.
Geo. A. Irvine.	John Wilkie.	Jas. A. Kilburn.
Bert Cox.	Thos. W. Atkinson.	Wm. A. Smith.
Wm. E. Snowden.	Jos. Cummings.	Arthur Stout.
Frank Hastings.	Wm. Callender.	Jos. Tyreman.
John Carroll.	Wm. Smith.	Francis W. Hay.
Fred Allen.	Wm. Eliott.	Jas. Randell.
Wm. Burgon.	Jackson Stonehouse.	Wm. T. Turnbull.
John Whitford.	Wm. J. Brown.	John Humphries.
Hy. Loach.	Alf Dove.	John Wilbraham.
Thos. R. Hopper.	Wm. E. Thompson.	Thomas Odell.
Wm. Raine.	Hy. Lee.	Alex Arbuckle.
Robt. Wilyman.	Geo. W. Wilkinson.	John Withers.
Wm. Lamplough.	Edw. Ibbetson.	Chris. Corner.
Wm. G. Anderson.	Thos. Smith.	Wm. H. Garnett.
Herbert J. Sayers.	Jos. W. Elgey.	Edw. Rowland.

Rich. Hayes.
Fred Canfield.
Michael R. Carr.
Frank Murry.
Samuel Payne.
Wm. Thompson.
Thomas Bunter.
Thomas D. Raine.
R. H. C. Horsley.
John Hewison.
David Holmes.
Wm. E. Orde.
Geo. J. Marshall.
Alf Greathead.
Geo. West.
Geo. Gofton.
John Wilkinson.
Norwood Denton.
Jas. T. Dalkin.
Hy. Davison.
Ernest Herbert.
Jos. Tidyman.
Anthony D. Short.
Thomas Clark.
Wm. Richardson.
Albert E. Dean.
Wm. Chapple.
Thos. Turnbull.
John Maiden.
Geo. Callen.
John H. Vart.
Ness Hodgson.
Thos. W. Cheetham.
Thos. Parish.
John Campbell.

John Stainthorpe.
W. G. Usher.
Hugh Ross.
Michael C. Johnson.
Andrew Hogg.
John Dent.
Hy. Lumsden.
Charles Measor.
Joseph Massey.
Jas. Heggie.
Harry Levett.
Geo. H. Atkinson.
Wm. Pegg.
T. J. Jobling.
L. Hanselman.
S. Holroyd.
J. T. Woods.
G. Pearson.
J. W. Cummings.
W. E. Williamson.
J. Harrison.
Hy. Fordham.
Jas. Mitchell.
Robt. A. Bolton.
Robt. A. Tate.
Alf Price.
M. J. Sparrow.
J. Oldfield.
J. G. Forcer.
M. Corner.
R. Massey.
B. Gummersall.
W. Rowntree.
J. Rowntree.
H. Lightfoot.
J. E. Sharp.

W. Key.
Wm. Robson.
A. F. Macknight.
Frank Gardner.
A. Dand.
J. W. Wilson.
R. P. Purves.
T. P. Metcalfe.
J. P. Tuck.
J. Docherty.
J. L. Newton.
J. Shevill.
Jas. Shingles.
E. Gray.
F. Bolton.
John H. R. Denton.
Jos. Charlton.
H. Tipple.
G. E. Watt.
L. Barnett.
A. H. Eve.
O. P. Mitchell.
J. W. Steel.
C. Appleby.
B. Metcalf.
Geo. Wardell.
J. H. Cloke.
Jos. H. Farrow.
B. Fell.
S. J. Wheatly.
Fred Snowdon.
W. P. Arkless.
J. Corbett.
W. Collings.
G. Davison.

In addition to the names given, many others assisted, both civilians and soldiers on furlough, whose names unfortunately have not been ascertained.

The Chief Constable's letter given on next page testifies to the efficient services rendered.

HARTLEPOOLS CITIZENS' TRAINING LEAGUE.

Dear Sir,

I shall be gratefully obliged if you will convey to the members of your League my high appreciation and thanks for their services in assisting the Police from the 16th to the 20th December, 1914, after the Bombardment, in the removal of the dead, succouring the wounded, the assistance rendered in the protection of property (which was exposed), and the regulation of the enormous amount of traffic.

During this trying period your members showed great tact in the performance of those duties.

My thanks are also due to you and your officers for the excellent arrangements which were carried out so well.

Yours faithfully,

A. WINTERBOTTOM, Chief Constable.

Commandant Smyth, J.P.,
Middlegate, Hartlepool.

This is a facsimile of the very neat and artistic badge presented to each special constable by the War Emergency Committee. It is on white metal, worked in silver and blue and brown enamel. The badge was designed by Councillor J. W. Boanson and executed by Messrs. Watkins, Ltd., Jewellers, West Hartlepool.

WEST HARTLEPOOL
WAR EMERGENCY COMMITTEE.

Special Constable Commander—
THE MAYOR (Councillor J. R. Fryer).
Hon. Secretary—
Mr. NELSON F. DENNIS, Borough Engineer.

The town was divided into eight districts or wards, each district having a member of the Committee acting as group leader, with about fifty special constables under his charge. Each district was further sub-divided into five sections, with a section leader and nine constables to each. Most of the constables were taken from the Citizens' Training League—President, J. R. Borrett; Treasurer, Chas. Longden; Secretary, Jas. Burdon. The following are the details:—

CENTRAL WARD.
Group Leader: Ald. Major R. MARTIN, V.D.

Section I.—Leader: T. White. Constables: D. Gough, J. Appleyard, G. Thompson, J. Smith, W. A. Liddle, W. E. Plummer, H. A. Sample, W. Smith, B. Henderson.

Section II.—Leader: A. Kenyon. Constables: F. Hill, H. C. Dewhirst, J. E. Romney, J. W. Dodsworth, T. Goodall, W. J. Smith, R. Baker.

Section III.—Leader: H. Calvert. Constables: H. Spurr, A. C. Oram, W. Hammond, D. Turnbull, R. Foster, H. Roberts, W. Wilson, R. W. Lee, A. Gregg, H. H. Geddes.

Section IV.—Leader: R. Downie. Constables: W. H. Morson, J. Bainbridge, M. S. Scurr, R. Hume, F. Marshall, J. B. Ormond, H. S. Clayton, J. Wright.

Section V.—Leader: J. W. Clark. Constables: C. D. King, J. B. Barker, E. Stephens, R. Robinson, H. Battison, F. Botham, A. T. Gyllenspetz.

Deputy Group Leader: H. Calvert. Despatch Rider: A. H. Barrett.

PARK WARD.

Group Leader: Councillor W. EDGAR.

Section I.—Leader: F. Witty. Constables: J. Barker, C. J. Blake, R. H. Harrison, S. Harrison, T. Heslop, W. H. W. Stephenson, F. L. Smith, E. W. Walker.

Section II.—Leader: J. B. Roberts. Constables: N. Andrews, J. Garner, R. Hood, T. A. Hodgson, R. E. Johnson, W. H. Tate, W. C. Watson, A. Watson, W. G. Whitehead.

Section III.—Leader: G. F. Wells. Constables: J. H. Austin, W. Bainbridge, J. W. Galley, J. H. Hutchinson, G. H. Pennock, T. W. Richardson, A. D. Scott, C. N. Vickers.

Section IV.—Leader: T. G. Dutton. Constables: J. W. Howey, W. Lawson, R. S. Renney, J. Robson, A. E. Scurr, B. W. Tilney, T. A. Taylor, G. H. Wheeler, J. Wilson.

Section V.—Leader: J. N. Reid. Constables: J. S. Kerridge, R. P. Glover, T. Forster, E. Langford, T. W. Maddison, S. Maddison, B. Moore, W. Robinson, W. H. Williams.

Scout Master: C. C. Waud. Hon. Secretary: A. Bowes.

WEST WARD.

Group Leader: A. B. HORSLEY, Esq., J.P.

Section I.—Leader: R. G. Boothby. Constables: S. T. Smurthwaite, J. Stangroom, R. W. Stangroom, J. W. Jefferson, C. H. Lyth, T. Young, H. M. Prestidge, J. Thompson, W. Dormand, D. T. Steel, R. Hoyle.

Section II.—Leader: J. J. Kinninmonth. Constables: R. Randall, P. R. Crawford, J. G. Harker, A. C. Prettyman, E. W. Railton, J. W. Jones, F. Thornton, G. Raine, S. Johnson, J. R. Dodsworth, W. Railton.

Section III.—Leader: F. H. Jackson. Constables: J. Gledden, A. Mathieson, R. Stephenson, J. Payne, W. Beavis, R. H. S. Whiting, J. T. Durkin, T. Mitchell, J. Hill, W. P. Dent.

Section IV.—Leader: D. Wilson. Constables: J. T. Rushton, J. W. Ridley, A. Smith, J. J. Rutherford, T. W. Hewitson, J. Blackburn, T. P. Robertson, J. A. Peck, W. Littlefair.

Section V.—Leader: W. Wilson. Constables: A. H. Cross, D. F. Ferguson, E. W. Witty, J. A. Blohm, J. W. Butcher, J. W. Sherwood, A. Roper, T. H. Warwick, C. Aspinall, K. Campbell.

Deputy Group Leader: F. H. Jackson.

SOUTH-WEST WARD.

Group Leader: Councillor J. W. BOANSON.

Section I.—T. Davidson. Constables: H. H. Birks, G. V. Arnold, J. W. Higgs, K. McLean, F. P. Howcroft, W. A. Stephenson, H. A. Dyer, W. Nelson, G. Ayre.

Section II.—Leader: R. H. Hodgson. Constables: T. B. Knight, J. Barker, D. W. Todd, A. V. Blackstone, W. Burgess, J. Burdon, N. Todd, W. Taylor, G. Fawcett, R. Fawcett, Councillor J. Hussey.

Section III.—Leader: F. Hogarth. Constables: J. Woodhall, A. Lovatt, E. Little, M. E. Fletcher, J. W. Ormond, W. Dodd, J. W. Emm, W. R. Story, W. J. Tucker.

Section IV.—Leader: J. W. Pratt. Constables: J. W. Shield, Thos. Oglesby, A. Blades, J. D. Stubbs, W. H. Bywater, J. W. Naylor, T. Gate, Chas. Graham.

Section V.—Leader: B. Grainger. Constables: E. M. Blyth, J. Boyle, W. T. Watson, S. Wright, H. White, S. Pearson, W. C. Holdforth, W. Burns, J. Fenton.

Hon. Secretary and Deputy Group Leader: R. H. Hodgson.

Despatch Rider: Preston Simpson.

NORTH-EAST WARD.

Group Leader: Councillor WM. JUBB COATES, Deputy Mayor.

Section I.—Leader: John Hardwick. Constables: W. G. Howard, Edgar Phillips, John Mitchell, Ed. Pringle, W. E. Piercy, F. Roe, J. Fothergill, T. W. Temple, Jos. Broster, D. A. Scott.

Section II.—Leader: F. C. Hewston. Constables: J. Arbuckle, D. Springgay, A. McWilliams, J. Craven, J. Kelley.

Section III.—Leader: E. P. Black. Constables: R. H. Lumley, J. C. Carswell, C. Kjelgaard, G. Grieveson, T. A. Dennison, J. Cooper, Jas. Mason.

Section IV.—Leader: T. Perry. Constables: R. Jacques, J. W. Stephenson, W. Robson, W. J. Greenleas, A. E. Cornley, J. Graham.

Section V.—Leader: J. K. Parsons. Constables: H. Whale, A. Bousfield, J. R. Richardson, C. Stephenson, J. McD. Fiddes, J. W. Bolton, R. Winter.

Hon. Secretary: Fred Morley.

SOUTH-EAST WARD.

Group Leader: Councillor W. T. RYAN.

Section I.—Leader: W. Smith. Constables: J. Currell, J. W. Cotson, R. Wainwright, A. Blakey, H. Pears, B. T. Jones, G. Andrews, T. Stamp, W. R. J. Chiverton.

Section II.—Leader: J. T. Dickinson. Constables: T. Daniel, J. W. Hetherington, J. Comb, T. Middlemiss, D. Petch, J. W. Richards, G. E. Holroyd, W. Gilfoyle.

Section III.—Leader: D. L. James. Constables: R. Gale, E. Edwards, R. Lamb, Jos. Cheney, C. E. Williams.

Section IV.—Leader: G. W. Cass. Constables: R. Outhwaite, G. H. Dickinson, C. Fowler, E. G. Judson, J. Kirby, R. V. Powell.

Deputy Group Leader: C. Longden. Hon. Secretary: S. S. Hewitson.

NORTH WARD.

Group Leader: Councillor T. F. THOMPSON.

Section I.—Leader: Hy. Gowing. Constables: Wm. Duthie, W. Firbank, H. P. Laidman, J. T. Atkinson, J. Howgego, J. Kingston, A. V. Roxborough, W. B. Howgego, J. P. Spoors.

Section II.—Leader: Jas. Howe. Constables: J. W. Thompson, J. D. Piper, S. Mailin, Jno. R. Rhea, W. Nightingale Hall, R. N. Ripley, F. J. Gibbs, G. T. Pearson, W. Ashton.

Section III.—Leader: S. M. Pease. Constables: S. Strover, E. M. P. Brown, M. McNeil, M. Irvin, J. F. Dawes, Thos. Doughty, A. O. Old, E. Hardy, Wm. Hudson.

Section IV.—Leader: W. Cameron. Constables: F. H. Lavin, F. Jackson, G. W. Greener, Wm. Hood, W. Inglis, John Wallace, C. T. Watson, R. H. Furby, H. McNeil, H. V. Garbutt.

Section V.—Leader: T. Leak. Constables: Wm. Neal, W. W. Foote, T. Alf Guy, R. Watson, Jas. Harrison, W. Ransford, J. R. Graham, B. Lawson, J. R. Borrett.

Hon. Secretary: Jos. Benn.

SEATON WARD (Seaton Carew Area).

Group Leader: Councillor E. O. BENNETT.

Sergeants: W. S. Lithgo, G. H. Stephenson, T. Gilbertson, C. F. Burton, W. M. Burns, C. Wainwright, S. Walker, E. J. White, J. McGowan.

Special Constables: J. Blenkinsop, J. Nicholson, R. Blackett, H. Chapman, T. B. Robinson, H. McNeil, J. E. Boddy, H. Burton, G. Mackay, R. Gales, W. Blackett, E. Harrison, J. Young, J. Hutton, J. Farrell, W. Waller, — Ostergard, T. J. Davies, H. J. Spence, F. W. Ferguson, C. Storey, J. Lithgo, T. Blenkinsop, E. Edwards, J. J. Stephenson, A. Forster, T. H. Tilly (junr.), F. L. Saniter, F. W. J. Webb, J. Hessler, C. Stebbings, H. D. Tate, J. H. Garry, E. Nicholson, J. Howlett, W. T. Morgan, H. Elders, R. Johnson, J. Bulmer, H. Lewis.

Deputy Group Leader: Councillor R. H. CHARLTON.

FOGGY FURZE AREA.

Group Leader: CHAS. CARTER.

Sergeant and Deputy Group Leader: Rev. W. J. Knowlden.

Sergeants: G. Fawcett, J. Sanderson.

Constables: R. Dobson, W. Martin, F. F. Smith, A. Warr, F. Elders, R. Barber, H. M. Arnold, J. Beal, T. W. Robinson, H. Armstrong, R. F. Willson, S. Jarman, H. Ambler, Coun. W. H. Thornton, J. Carr, W. Ransford, W. Tittle, T. Lowery, J. Hughes, D. Rowell, R. Walker, A. E. Ridley, A. J. Lambert, C. A. Pearse, E. Thomas, T. Teasdale, T. W. Ashton, D. Thomas, T. Bendelow, Coun. A. Casper, J. Horgan, A. Glendenning.

After the bombardment, the following instructions were printed on cards and delivered by the special constables from house to house in West Hartlepool:—

COUNTY BOROUGH OF WEST HARTLEPOOL

PRECAUTIONARY NOTICE ONLY.

Re Bombardment or Hostile Landing.

The inhabitants are requested to read the following INSTRUCTIONS, issued for their assistance and guidance, so that in the event of further BOMBARDMENT or attempted INVASION (which are considered unlikely) they may BE PREPARED.

IN THE CASE OF BOMBARDMENT.

1. KEEP INSIDE. Go into cellar, or bottom room farthest from direction of shell fire, and away from windows or glass. Don't rush into street, congregate, or watch the firing from any exposed position. If possible, turn off the gas meter, to obviate burning in case of building being struck.

2. SEEK SHELTER at nearest substantial building, if you are in the street during Bombardment, or when Aircraft is seen or heard.

IN THE CASE OF HOSTILE LANDING.

3. KEEP INSIDE (unless ordered to leave), and act as directed in Instruction No. 1.

4. IF YOU LEAVE, use only the Roads pointed out by the Special Constables.
   Proceed quickly and orderly. Don't gather in crowds, or rush to Railway Station. Take what clothing and food you can carry. It is recommended that you wrap a blanket round yourself and children, and bring away all umbrellas.

5. VEHICLES, not required by the Military, will be used for the conveyance of aged and infirm persons and young children only.

6. COLLECTING AREA selected is Sedgefield. The Special Constables will give directions as to the roads to traverse. A Committee of Group Leaders will be at the "Collecting Area" to make such arrangements to minimise as much as possible the inconvenience that may arise during the short time the refugees would have to remain.

APPLYING TO BOTH DANGERS.

7. SPECIAL CONSTABLES will be posted at suitable points to direct pedestrian and other traffic, and attention to their orders will prevent panic. If you are obliged, and permitted, to go towards the town, keep to streets running parallel with, and on nearest footpath to, the sea.

8. REMEMBER TO KEEP COOL, in order that by example you may help those around you to be calmed.
   Don't repeat, but discourage alarmist talk.
   Give information of any person or persons circulating alarmist reports likely to create a scare.

9. UNEXPLODED SHELLS, or bombs, should not be touched, as they may burst if moved. Inform the Military, as soon as this can safely be done, where they are.

10. FIREARMS. The inhabitants are strongly advised not to carry or be in possession of firearms.

11. The "GROUP LEADERS" are as follows:—

> Central Ward—Ald. R. Martin.
> North Ward—Coun. T. F. Thompson.
> South-East Ward—Coun. W. T. Ryan.
> Seaton Ward—Coun. E. O. Bennett.
> North-East Ward—Coun. W. J. Coates.
> Park Ward—Coun. W. Edgar.
> South-West Ward—Coun. J. W. Boanson.
> West Ward—A. B. Horsley, Esq.

> N. F. DENNIS, Hon. Secretary.

By Order,

> J. R. FRYER (Mayor),

> Special Constable Commander.

PROCLAMATION.

NAVAL BOMBARDMENT

The Civil Population are requested, as far as possible, to keep to their houses for the present. The situation is now secure.

The Group Leaders of each Ward will advise in case of further danger.

Any unexploded shells must not be touched, but information as to the position thereof given to the nearest Police Officer, or to the Police Station.

J. R. FRYER,

Mayor.

Dated the 16th day of December, 1914.

GOD SAVE THE KING.

GREAT WAR MEMOIRS, BIOGRAPHIES

Not for nothing has the First World War gone down in history as the most literate, and literary, ever fought. The products of mass education went into action en masse for the first time, and in the case of junior officers, the products of classical education went too. The result was an unprecedented mass of written material from the trenches. This a selection from our published stock that cover both sides of the wire.

MEDAL WITHOUT BAR
An English War Novel
Richard Blaker
9781783314249

1916-1918 A WAR DIARY
By H M Adams MC Worcester Regt.
9781783317271

THE ADVANCE FROM MONS 1914
By Walter Bloem with a Foreword by Sir James E. Edmonds
9781783317523

MY .75
REMINISCENCES OF A GUNNER OF A 75M/M BATTERY
By Paul Lintier
9781783317936

IRON TIMES WITH THE GUARDS
By an "O. E." (Pseudonym of Lt. G. P. A. Fildes, Coldstream Guards)
9781783312924

MERRY HELL! A DANE WITH THE CANADIANS
By Thomas Dinesen, VC
9781845740962

GUN FODDER
A DIARY OF FOUR YEARS OF WAR
by A.Hamilton Gibbs
9781845741686

OLD SOLDIERS NEVER DIE
By Frank Richards, DCM, MM.
9781843420262

LANGEMARCK AND CAMBRAI
By Capt Geoffrey Dugdale
9781845742683

MY WAR MEMORIES 1914-1918
By General Ludendorff
9781845743031

A BRIGADIER IN FRANCE
By Hanway R.Cumming
9781843421320

OVER THE TOP. A "P.B.I." in the H.A.C
By Arthur Lambert
9781843421269

AT G.H.Q.
By Brigadier General John Charteris CMG DSO
9781474538039